LOW-FAT GRILLING

〜 〜 〜 〜 〜 〜 〜 〜 〜 〜 〜 〜 〜

Also by Melanie Barnard:

Sunday Suppers (with Brooke Dojny)
Let's Eat In (with Brooke Dojny)
Parties! (with Brooke Dojny)
Cheap Eats (with Brooke Dojny)
The Best Covered and Kettle Grills Cookbook Ever

LOW-FAT GRILLING

Fabulous Food from the Backyard Barbecue

Melanie Barnard

HarperPerennial

A Division of HarperCollins*Publishers*

HarperCollins books may be purchased for educational, business, or sales promotional use. For information, please write: Special Markets Department, HarperCollins Publishers, Inc., 10 East 53rd Street, New York, NY 10022.

FIRST EDITION

Designed by Nancy Singer

Library of Congress Cataloging-in-Publication Data

Barnard, Melanie.
    Low-fat grilling / Melanie Barnard. — 1st ed.
        p.   cm.
    Includes index.
    ISBN 0-06-095073-0
    1. Barbecue cookery. 2. Low-fat diet—Recipes. I. Title.
TX840.B3B373   1995
641.7'6—dc20   94-33253

95 96 97 98 99 ❖/RRD 10 9 8 7 6 5 4 3 2 1

*For Susan, who definitely knows a good barbecued
brisket when she sees one*

CONTENTS

〜 〜 〜 〜 〜 〜 〜 〜 〜

ACKNOWLEDGMENTS

‍ ‍ ‍ ‍ ‍ ‍ ‍ ‍ ‍

Many people provided inspiration for this book, especially my editor, Susan Friedland, who accompanied me on a Texas barbecue odyssey, and Ron Snider, who led us on the tour. My husband, Scott, and my sons, Dave, Jeff, and Matt, are all avid grilling enthusiasts, willing tasters, and kindly but forthright critics. Brooke Dojny, my longtime colleague, is also my most trusted and valued culinary friend, whose honest opinions continue to keep me on track. Bob Cornfield, my excellent agent, is a major source of quietly consistent support.

Recipes must work succesfully on a variety of cooking grills, including gas and charcoal, as well as smokers for certain recipes. Special thanks go to the grill manufacturers who provided equipment for testing: the New Braunfels Smoker Company, Char-Broil, and the Ducane Company.

Complete and accurate nutritional data are of utmost importance in a book such as this. Lynne and William Hill of Hill Nutrition Associates, Inc., provided expert guidance and professional nutritional analysis on all of the recipes.

INTRODUCTION

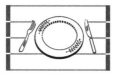

Grilling is both the oldest and newest method of cookery. Harken back to those old textbooks where a hairy-chested caveman is depicted spearing his recently clubbed wild boar over a glowing open wood fire. Then refer to a slick, trendy contemporary food magazine and note the hairy-chested city man cooking his recently purchased free-range chicken over glowing mesquite charcoal. Not all that much has changed.

There are a lot of reasons why grilling has remained so popular for these thousands of years. First, being out of doors is the logical way to cook in the summer. Even the man in the textbook figured out that escaping the cave was the thing to do on a hot day. In addition, it's the easy way out. Grilling all but eliminates the scrubbing of pots and pans, which was probably particularly irksome when water had

1

to be lugged from the melting glacier. Most important, grilled foods taste good. Even a tough old boar takes on a deliciously different dimension, and grilling does similarly great things for today's favorite foods.

But it was while writing another book on grilling, *The Best Kettle and Covered Grills Cookbook Ever,* that I first realized grilling was also a great solution to the very modern problem of reducing fat in our diets.

About halfway through the book, during a summer when we ate little but the results of the day's grill "tests," I noticed that my shopping and our eating habits were changing. The bags contained almost no butter, and a lot less oil than usual. In addition, I found myself buying and portioning out less meat than my husband and three grown sons would have ever accepted in the past.

Grilling was making the difference in the way we were eating. Whereas lots of oil is needed for deep-frying, and the flavor of browned butter is integral to the success of many sautéed dishes, grilled foods require little or no added fat of any kind, and instead take most of their taste cues from the cooking method itself.

It became clear that the grill is a perfect way to cook low-fat meals. Instead of making major taste sacrifices and substituting weird ingredients or time-consuming cooking methods to render foods "low-fat," the grill was doing the job naturally, efficiently, and deliciously.

I really do love eating good food, and am inherently suspicious of deprivation diets that smack of "Eat it, it's good for you," since, in my experience, that old saw usually refers to things no one would eat for any other reason. On the other hand, I am concerned for my family, my readers, and myself in light of the wealth of substantiated data supporting a low-fat diet for better health and well-being.

The basic elements of a sound diet are moderation and variety. Moderation means balancing high- and low-fat foods to an average that remains within the currently accepted guidelines of less than 30 percent of all calories taken in as fat. Variety means eating lots of different foods for the most interesting tastes and broad intake of important nutrients. An informed approach to moderation and variety with an emphasis on great flavor, rather than a boring and tasteless enslavement to pure numbers, is the key to living low-fat and loving it.

The recipes in this book have nutritional coding to help you serve them in a context of overall healthy eating. The total number of calories and grams of fat per serving are given, as well as the percentage of calories obtained from fat. In every case, this is less than 30 percent, which is the generally accepted nutritional guideline for good health. To further aid in meal planning, amounts of sodium, carbohydrate, protein, saturated fat, and cholesterol are given for each serving. Remember that the meal can be made even lower in fat by serving side dishes with negligible fat content, such as wide varieties of fruits and vegetables—all of which taste terrific with grilled foods!

My philosophy on low-fat cooking is the same as in all my cooking. Start with the best and freshest ingredients, whether it is a quality chicken breast or an ear of corn from the farm stand, and then prepare them with simplicity for good taste. Grilling is a fabulously easy and naturally delicious way to do just that—and to lower the fat in our diet too.

The guy in the cave was no dummy.

HOW LOW-FAT GRILLING WORKS

- *When a well-seasoned grill rack is lightly coated with a nonstick vegetable spray before cooking, even boneless chicken breasts can be successfully grilled with no added fat.*

- *Marinades, which rely on acid and intense seasonings and need little or no fat, can tenderize lean cuts of meat as well as add terrific flavor.*

- *The direct heat of the fire serves to caramelize the natural carbohydrates in vegetables and fruits, and even in meats and poultry.*

- *The smoke, especially if aromatic woods and/or herbs are tossed onto the coals, lends fabulous taste to foods.*

- *Fat in meats and poultry drips away during grilling.*

- *Many vegetables take on a woodsy flavor and meaty texture when grilled, and are so deliciously satisfying that they can become a meal in themselves.*

GRILLING BASICS

TYPES OF GRILLS

The home cooking grill, defined as a unit with a metal box for fuel and a grid for cooking the meat, comes in dozens of varieties on the basic theme. For the most part, however, grills can be divided into covered or uncovered, and charcoal or gas.

These days, with the exception of little portable hibachis for the beach, the vast majority of grills sold is the covered type. A covered grill is far more efficient and predictable than an uncovered grill, or brazier, which allows large quantities of heat to escape and is subject to variations from wind and temperature conditions. Consequently, a covered grill uses less fuel and forms a more controlled cooking environment, both of which mean better cooking results.

Home smokers also fall in the covered grill category. Especially useful are those designed with a fire built in a small box that is vented into a larger cooking box, creating the heat and smoke for cooking and flavoring. They are especially versatile since direct and indirect grilling as well as smoking can be done simultaneously.

There is really no flavor replacement for charcoal-fired cooking, but the high-quality gas grills on the market today produce good results. Their advantages are speed and ease. The more innovative designs almost replicate the smoky flavor imparted by cooking over charcoal. Whereas charcoal fires are generally messy and take at least 30 minutes to get started, gas grills operate just like your kitchen stove. Simply turn on the gas and preheat about 10 minutes. Depending upon the manufacturer, cooking "coals" or grids maximize the smoke produced during cooking, and special wood chips (available in mesquite, hickory, or fruitwood) enhance flavors. At our house, we use both charcoal and gas grills. The recipes in this book, except where specifically noted, will work on either one.

Electric grills, although improved in the last couple of years, are not as sophisticated or satisfactory, but are well suited to small spaces where gas or charcoal would create a ventilation problem.

Whether you use a gas, charcoal, or electric grill, the grids provide the cooking surface. They should be set wide enough apart to allow for maximum heat and smoke circulation, but narrow enough so that foods will not fall through. Certain items, such as sliced vegetables or small pieces of meat or seafood, may need to be grilled on a skewer or on a special grill rack insert or screen that can easily be fitted to almost any grill. Hinged rack containers for fish or sliced vegetables make turning of small pieces much easier. These are widely available at moderate cost.

COOKING FUELS

Hardwood or Lump Charcoal. Made by slowly burning hardwood chunks under controlled, oxygen-free conditions that reduce the wood to carbon, this is my favorite cooking fuel since it contains no additives and burns both clean and long. It is relatively expensive and hard to come by, but as grilling becomes more popular, so does the availbilty of good hardwood charcoal.

Charcoal Briquets. The most widely used grilling fuel, briquets are efficient, readily available, and inexpensive. Like hardwood charcoal, briquets are made by smoldering wood into carbon. But the wood is often compressed with starch binders, and often mixed with sawdust and wood scraps; many manufacturers add other chemicals, such as nitrites, to promote quick ignition. When the fire is properly built, allowing at least 30 minutes for the briquets to burn off the chemical additives, there is usually no aftertaste in the food.

Hardwood. This is what the guy in the cave probably used, and it still works well today, though it is used less frequently, since hardwood is harder to ignite, burns quickly, and gives off a less predictable heat than charcoal. Oak, hickory, fruitwood, and mesquite are the most common cooking hardwoods. Their flavor can also be imparted by the use of wet wood chips tossed onto a charcoal fire.

Gas. Gas grills can be fired by permanent underground pipelines or by portable, usually propane, tanks. Both work very well.

AROMATIC ADDITIONS

Wood Chips and Chunks. Wood chips, well soaked in water and tossed onto hot coals, produce highly aromatic smoke that permeates food as it cooks. Chunks are hardwoods that can be added to charcoal to be used as a flavorful adjunct fuel. Used judiciously, both chips and chunks can add an unparalleled depth of flavor to grilled foods. The trick is to pair the right wood to the food.

- **Hickory.** *The distinct, heavily smoky, bacon flavor is best suited to assertive meats such as pork and beef.*

- **Mesquite.** *As charcoal, mesquite burns a bit hotter than other fuels. As chips, it produces a subtle yet characteristically woodsy smoke that enhances most meats and poultry, and especially fish.*

- **Fruitwoods.** *The most common are cherry, apple, and peach. All give off subtle fruity aromas, which are especially good with poultry, pork, and veal, and with recipes that include grilled fruit.*

Grapevine Twigs and Cuttings. These give a subtle, winey flavor to fish, poultry, vegetables, and fruits.

Fresh Herbs. Dampened fresh herbs and branches reflecting recipe ingredients can be tossed onto hot coals just before cooking for subtle flavor enhancement.

Preparing the Best Charcoal Fire

Use plenty of charcoal so that the bed is 2 or 3 inches deep and at least 2 inches larger in circumference than the area needed for the food to be cooked. Depending upon the fire starter method used, the coals may first need to be heaped in a pyramid, then spread out when hot and you are ready to grill.

Most home grilling is done over a **direct** fire, with the food cooked on the grill rack directly over the hot coals. Some foods, notably those that need long, slower cooking or that are more delicate, do better with an **indirect** fire. This is easily obtained by preparing the fire as usual, then, with tongs, pushing the coals to the perimeter or to one side of the firebox. The food to be cooked is placed on the grill rack in the area away from the hot coals.

Starter Methods (in order of my preference)

Gas Igniters. With the ease of pressing a button, these spark the prepared charcoal. They are available as options on several sophisticated charcoal grills, and butane igniters can be purchased separately.

Electric Fire Starters. A metal loop element inserted into the center of a pyramid of coals takes about 10 minutes to heat the adjacent coals red hot. The lit coals then ignite the remaining coals in the pyramid, in another 10 or 15 minutes. Be sure to cool the element on a heat-proof surface well away from people and pets. The obvious drawback here is that the grill must be near an electric outlet.

Chimney Starter. Crumpled newspaper is stuffed into the bottom of this perforated metal cylinder, and charcoal is piled into the top. Set the cylinder into the grill firebox and ignite the newspaper, which will in turn ignite the charcoal in about 20 minutes. If additional coals are needed, they can be added to the prepared fire.

Fluid and Solid Fuel Starters. These contain combustible chemicals. Fluids should be squirted onto unlit charcoal, and solid starter blocks placed on the bottom of a pyramid of unlit charcoal. The starter is carefully ignited, and then burned at least 30 minutes to allow the chemicals to dissipate. Do not add chemical starters to an already lit fire.

THE COOKING TEMPERATURE

It usually takes about 30 minutes to get a proper charcoal fire going. The temperature of the coals will never be as well controlled as in a gas grill but in a covered grill the heat can be raised or lowered by opening or closing the lid and vents. Remember that oxygen is a major component in a fire, so the less oxygen allowed to reach the flame, the lower the heat. Read the directions for your grill for specific instructions on controlling the fire. Cooking temperature can also be varied by raising or lowering the grill rack in relation to the hot coals.

Grilling is, at best, an imprecise cooking method. Most of the recipes in this book call for medium or medium-hot coals, but to allow for climate and grill variables, a range of cooking times is provided in most cases. Check for doneness after the minimum time. General guidelines for testing fire temperatures are as follows:

- *Hot. The coals glow red and you can hold your hand 6 inches above the fire for no more than 3 seconds. Temperature range is between 425° and 475° F. Good for searing meat and fish.*

- *Medium-hot. The coals are gray with a red underglow and you can hold your hand 6 inches above the coals for no more than 5 seconds. Temperature range is between 375° and 425° F. Good for most poultry and meats.*

- *Medium. The coals are gray with only a hint of red and you can hold your hand 6 inches above the fire for no more than 7 seconds. Temperature range is between 325° and 375° F. Good for most fruits, vegetables, and delicate seafood or poultry.*

- *Low. The coals are completely gray and you can hold your hand 6 inches above the fire for 10 seconds. Temperature range is 275° to 325° F. Good for warming rolls and delicate fruits.*

GRILL SAFETY

Position the grill in an open area well away from the house, dry leaves, or combustibles.

Do not leave a grill unattended. Wind, dogs, and children can easily knock it over.

Never add starter fluid or solid starters after the fire has been started.

Keep a fire extinguisher, bucket of sand, or source of water nearby.

Check coals for several hours after cooking in a grill and up to 48 hours in a smoker to be sure they are completely extinguished.

Turn off the gas at the source after each use of a gas grill.

When grilling, do not wear loose or flowing clothing that can catch the flames, nor dangling jewelry that will heat up and perhaps cause burns.

If using a marinade as a table sauce, first boil it for 3 minutes to destroy bacteria that may have been present during marinating of the raw ingredients.

GRILLING TIPS

Lightly coat the grill rack with a nonstick vegetable spray before setting in place over the coals.

Allow the grill rack to heat at least 5 minutes over the hot coals before using. Foods tend to stick to a cold rack.

Trim all excess fat from meats and poultry, not only to lower the fat content but to reduce the chance of grill flare-ups.

Turn foods with tongs or a spatula while grilling to avoid piercing them and thus losing juices.

Brush on thick or sweet sauces mostly during the last 5 or 10 minutes of grilling time to prevent burning.

Be careful not to overcook lean meats, poultry, and seafood. Poultry needs to be thoroughly cooked until white throughout and seafood cooked until opaque, but the food will quickly dry out after that.

Look for reduced-sodium broths, soy sauces, and other condiments. They can give a great flavor punch without an overdose of salt.

Use fresh herbs if you can, especially basil, cilantro, thyme, marjoram, tarragon, and rosemary, which are far better fresh than dried. If using dried herbs or spices, be sure they are still pungent enough to impart flavor. Store them in small quantities in a cool cupboard for no more than about 6 months. After that, they will lose potency.

Make attractive and professional-looking cross-hatch grill marks by searing meats or fish over a hot fire on a hot grill rack for about 2 minutes. Rotate the food about 45 degrees and grill 2 minutes more. Turn over and repeat the process on the other side.

APPETIZERS

Except for a plate of boring raw vegetables, low-fat, good-tasting appetizers and snacks are hard to come by. Unless it's a cocktail party where the nibbles are the only food offered, most people think of snacks last in menu planning. This is good for the potato chip and salted peanuts industries, which have built empires on quick, easy, and universally popular snack fare. However, these are also high in fat and low in originality.

On the other hand, grilling just about anything, even simple potato slices or a variation on a classic salsa, elevates the ordinary into the exotic. The woodsy fragrance of the fire and the tasty, lightly charred edges of these foods more than make up for the deep-fried flavor that is the main attraction of many other appetizers. Fresh vegetables and naturally low-fat seafood, especially when paired with intense seasonings, make fabulous grilled appetizers.

For a small party, grilled appetizers make most sense when the main course is also to be cooked on the grill, allowing the fire to do double duty. For a large gathering, especially a cocktail party, grilled tidbits and snacks alone make firing up the grill worthwhile. Little brochettes of ultra-spicy shrimp on a smoking grill set off to the corner of the patio (downwind of the party, please) or a grilled antipasta with fragrant aioli dipping sauce are certain to draw out a reticent crowd, and home-smoked trout or yeasty grilled pizzas are exotic enough to cause quite a stir, even among the most jaded guests.

The trick is to build the fire early enough and have enough coals on hand to keep it for the entire time you plan on using it. If your party is really large, you might hire a competent teenager to do the actual cooking, which will leave you free to have fun at your own party.

≀≀≀ Grilled Basil Polenta 14

≀≀≀ Smoked Trout on Sesame Melba Toast 15

≀≀≀ Grilled Gravlax-Style Salmon 16

≀≀≀ Grilled Hoisin and Ginger Swordfish Tidbits 18

≀≀≀ Seared Tuna and Roasted Pepper Antipasto 19

≀≀≀ Grilled Sea Scallops with Papaya-Curry Dipping Sauce 21

≀≀≀ Jerked Shrimp 22

≀≀≀ Grilled Clams with Fresh Horseradish Salsa 24

≀≀≀ Grilled White Clam Pizza 25

≀≀≀ Grilled Antipasto Vegetables with Elephant Garlic Aioli 26

≀≀≀ Grilled Corn and Tomato Salsa 28

≀≀≀ Grilled Tomato and Basil Pizzas 29

≀≀≀ Grilled Honey Mustard Sweet Potato Thins 31

≀≀≀ Grilled Potato "Chips" 32

≀≀≀ Grilled Caponata Crostini 33

≀≀≀ Curried Grilled Vegetables 35

GRILLED BASIL POLENTA

16 pieces

This is so good that you might want to make a whole meal of it. Such fresh herbs as thyme or rosemary or marjoram can be substituted for the basil.

2 cups reduced-sodium chicken broth
1 cup polenta or yellow cornmeal
1 cup cold water
2 teaspoons plus 1 tablespoon extra-virgin olive oil
¼ cup freshly grated Parmesan
¼ cup chopped or slivered fresh basil leaves
½ teaspoon salt
½ teaspoon freshly ground black pepper
2 cups low-fat bottled marinara sauce

In a 2-quart saucepan over medium heat, bring the broth to a boil. Whisk the polenta into the cold water, then slowly whisk the mixture into the boiling broth. Reduce the heat to low and cook, stirring almost constantly, until the mixture is very thick and pulls away from the side of the pan, about 13 to 15 minutes. Stir in 2 teaspoons oil, the cheese, basil, salt, and pepper.

Coat a 7- by 11-inch baking dish with nonstick vegetable spray. Spread the polenta evenly in the prepared dish. Let cool, then refrigerate at least 1 hour or up to 24 hours, until firm.

Prepare a medium barbecue fire. Oil the grill rack or coat with a nonstick vegetable spray. Cut the polenta into 16 rectangles and rub each gently with 1 tablespoon of the oil. In a saucepan, bring the marinara sauce to a simmer.

Grill the polenta, turning each piece once carefully with a spatula, until browned and crisp, 5 to 7 minutes total.

Serve the polenta on a platter with a bowl of the warm marinara sauce for dipping.

CALORIES	64.66 KCAL	PROTEIN	2.17 GM
TOTAL FAT	2.19 GM	SATURATED FAT	.50 GM
SODIUM	272.44 MG	CHOLESTEROL	1.20 MG
CARBOHYDRATE	9.33 GM		

% calories from fat: 29.99%

SMOKED TROUT ON SESAME MELBA TOAST

ʒ ʒ ʒ ʒ ʒ ʒ ʒ ʒ ʒ

6 to 8 appetizer servings

This recipe also appears in *The Best Covered and Kettle Grill Book Ever,* but it bears repeating since it is terrific and my expert griller husband is locally famous for the development of the smoking method. Don't gussy it up with fancy greenery or exotic herbs; this is plain and simple cooking at its best. Note that a covered charcoal grill is required.

2 whole fresh boned rainbow trout (each 10 to 12 ounces)
¼ cup coarse sea salt or kosher salt
2 or 3 handfuls hickory chips
Parsley sprigs for garnish
Sesame melba toasts

Rinse the trout in cold water. In a large bowl or crock, dissolve the salt in about 2 quarts of water. Add the trout and additional water to

continued

cover them if necessary. Cover the bowl and refrigerate the trout 24 hours. (The fish will firm up in the brine.)

Prepare a medium barbecue fire in a covered charcoal grill, then push the hot coals to the side to form an indirect fire. Oil the grill rack or coat with a nonstick vegetable spray. Soak the hickory chips in water to cover at least 30 minutes.

Remove the fish from the brine, rinse under cold water, then pat dry on paper toweling. Using a sharp knife, remove the heads and slit the trout along the center of the back to butterfly each fish.

Just before cooking, toss the wet hickory chips onto the coals. Place the trout, skin side down, on the side of the grill away from the coals. Cover the grill and smoke 40 minutes without opening the lid.

Present the freshly smoked trout on a platter garnished with the parsley sprigs and the crackers surrounding the fish. Use forks to pick off small pieces of the trout to eat on the crackers.

CALORIES	71.40 KCAL	PROTEIN	12.45 GM
TOTAL FAT	2.30 GM	SATURATED FAT	.39 GM
SODIUM	646.99 MG	CHOLESTEROL	34.53 MG
CARBOHYDRATE	.00 GM		

% calories from fat: 26.84%

GRILLED GRAVLAX-STYLE SALMON

8 to 10 appetizer servings

Gravlax, the classic dill-salt-and-sugar-cured salmon from Sweden, is the flavor inspiration here. The traditional accompaniments of lemon wedges, sour cream, and pumpernickel bread are also delicious with this grilled version.

1½ pounds skinned salmon fillets
1 tablespoon vegetable oil, preferably canola oil
1 teaspoon salt
1 teaspoon sugar
⅓ cup chopped fresh dill
½ cup low-fat or nonfat sour cream
1 teaspoon small drained capers
Dill sprigs
Lemon wedges
36 slices party rye bread

Prepare a medium-hot barbecue fire. Oil the grill rack or coat with a non-stick vegetable spray.

Rub the salmon with the oil, then sprinkle evenly with the salt and sugar. Sprinkle with the dill, patting it in to adhere. Grill the fish, turning once, 8 to 10 minutes, until it is just cooked through. Let the fish cool, then slice thinly. (The fish can be grilled early in the day.)

Stir together the sour cream and capers. Let stand at least 15 minutes or refrigerate up to 6 hours.

To serve, overlap slices of fish on a platter. Garnish with dill sprigs and lemon wedges. Serve at room temperature accompanied by the sour cream and bread slices.

CALORIES	156.58 KCAL	PROTEIN	12.54 GM
TOTAL FAT	4.99 GM	SATURATED FAT	.71 GM
SODIUM	375.36 MG	CHOLESTEROL	26.91 MG
CARBOHYDRATE	14.58 GM		

% calories from fat: 29.27%

Grilled Hoisin and Ginger Swordfish Tidbits

〜 〜 〜 〜 〜 〜 〜 〜 〜

8 to 10 appetizer servings

The thick sweetness of hoisin sauce is offset by the rice vinegar and soy sauce in this pungent Asian-style marinade. Fresh ginger and dried pepper flakes add the heat to these spicy preprandial tidbits. I like this appetizer cooked and served on small bamboo skewers, each with a couple of chunks of swordfish and a scallion. For a main course, cut the fish chunks into slightly larger pieces or leave the steaks intact before marinating and cooking. Tuna steaks make an excellent alternative to swordfish.

¼ cup hoisin sauce
2 tablespoons reduced-sodium soy sauce
1½ tablespoons rice wine vinegar
1 tablespoon dry sherry
2 cloves garlic, minced
2 tablespoons grated fresh ginger
¼ teaspoon dried hot red pepper flakes
1½ pounds swordfish steaks, cut into rough ¾-inch cubes
2 bunches slender scallions (about 20), trimmed to leave 2 inches of
  green part

In a shallow dish just large enough to hold the tuna and scallions, combine the hoisin sauce, soy sauce, vinegar, sherry, garlic, ginger, and pepper flakes. Add the swordfish, stirring to coat completely. Let stand 30 minutes. Add the scallions, stirring to coat, and let stand an additional 15 minutes.

Prepare a medium-hot barbecue fire. Oil the grill rack or coat with a nonstick vegetable spray. If using bamboo skewers, soak them in cold water to cover at least 30 minutes.

Thread the swordfish and scallions onto metal or soaked bamboo skewers, placing the scallions at the ends of the skewers. Grill, turning once or twice, about 6 minutes, until the fish is just cooked through and the scallions are lightly charred and softened.

CALORIES	101.13 KCAL	PROTEIN	14.26 GM
TOTAL FAT	2.80 GM	SATURATED FAT	.75 GM
SODIUM	251.08 MG	CHOLESTEROL	26.36 MG
CARBOHYDRATE	4.03 GM		

% calories from fat: 25.62%

SEARED TUNA AND ROASTED PEPPER ANTIPASTO

ι ι ι ι ι ι ι ι ι

10 appetizer or 5 main course servings

This is a lovely make-ahead first course for a sophisticated party. It is also a terrific and easy main course for a warm summer evening. Grill the tuna first, when the coals are red hot, then let them burn down a bit to roast the peppers.

¾ pound tuna steak, cut about ¼ inch thick
¾ teaspoon coarsely ground black pepper
¼ teaspoon salt
1 red bell pepper
1 yellow bell pepper
1 tablespoon extra-virgin olive oil
1 bunch arugula
2 teaspoons fresh lemon juice
1½-ounce piece Parmigiano-Reggiano, at room temperature
2 tablespoons drained small capers
Lemon wedges for garnish
1 French baguette or slim Italian loaf (about 10 ounces), thinly sliced

continued

Prepare a hot barbecue fire. Oil the grill rack or coat with a nonstick vegetable spray.

Sprinkle the tuna with ½ teaspoon of the pepper and the salt, patting it in to adhere. When the coals are hot, grill the tuna, turning once, 5 to 6 minutes, until lightly charred on the outside and just cooked through. The meat should have a trace of pink in the center. Let the fish cool to room temperature.

Let the coals burn down to medium temperature.

Cut the bell peppers into quarters and rub with 1 teaspoon of the oil. Grill the peppers, turning occasionally, 8 to 10 minutes, until softened. Peel off and discard most of the charred skin. (Tuna and peppers can be grilled early in the day and refrigerated. Return to room temperature to serve.)

To assemble the antipasto, cut the tuna on the bias into ¼-inch slices and thinly slice the peppers. Make a bed of arugula on a platter. Arrange the tuna and peppers, overlapping, on the arugula. Sprinkle with the remaining ¼ teaspoon pepper, remaining 2 teaspoons oil, and the lemon juice. Use a vegetable peeler to shave the cheese into thin slices. Scatter the cheese and capers over the antipasto. Garnish with the lemon wedges and serve at room temperature with the bread.

CALORIES	155.66 KCAL	PROTEIN	11.61 GM
TOTAL FAT	4.84 GM	SATURATED FAT	.76 GM
SODIUM	318.21 MG	CHOLESTEROL	14.90 MG
CARBOHYDRATE	16.02 GM		

% calories from fat: 28.27%

GRILLED SEA SCALLOPS WITH PAPAYA-CURRY DIPPING SAUCE

ι ι ι ι ι ι ι ι ι

8 to 10 appetizer servings

Grilled shrimp are also excellent with this Caribbean-inspired sauce. It is a fine dip for raw fruits or cocktail shrimp, too. Be sure to use ripe papayas that are soft enough to puree well.

1 medium papaya, peeled and seeded
1 large clove garlic, chopped
1 jalapeño, finely chopped
2 tablespoons dark rum
2 tablespoons fresh lime juice
1½ tablespoons white wine vinegar
1½ teaspoons chopped fresh thyme or ½ teaspoon dried
1 teaspoon curry powder
½ teaspoon salt
1½ pounds sea scallops
1 tablespoon vegetable oil, preferably canola oil
Salt and freshly ground black pepper
¼ cup chopped cilantro

Cut the papaya into chunks and place in a food processor along with the garlic and jalapeño. Process to a coarse puree. Add the rum, lime juice, vinegar, thyme, curry powder, and salt. Process to a smooth puree. Reserve at room temperature up to 1 hour or refrigerate up to 6 hours, then return to room temperature to serve.

Prepare a medium-hot barbecue fire. Oil the grill rack or coat with a nonstick vegetable spray. If using bamboo skewers, soak in

continued

cold water to cover at least 30 minutes. Rub the scallops with the oil, then season lightly with salt and pepper. Thread the scallops on metal or soaked bamboo skewers. Grill, turning once or twice, about 5 minutes, until just cooked through.

Sprinkle the scallops with the cilantro and serve with the dipping sauce.

CALORIES	103.66 KCAL	PROTEIN	12.97 GM
TOTAL FAT	2.15 GM	SATURATED FAT	.17 GM
SODIUM	245.38 MG	CHOLESTEROL	24.97 MG
CARBOHYDRATE	5.87 GM		

% calories from fat: 20.43%

JERKED SHRIMP

ι ι ι ι ι ι ι ι ι

8 appetizer or 4 main course servings

The "jerked" meats and poultry of Jamaica are "hot stuff" to trendy palates. Jumbo shrimp, with its meaty texture, is a nontraditional but definitely delicious variation on the theme. A mix of hot and sweet herbs and spices, the jerk seasoning can be either a liquid marinade or, as is used here, a rub. I especially like the addition of curry powder to the already complex blend of herbs and spices. Any unused spice mix can be stored, tightly covered, in a cool place for a couple of months.

1 teaspoon dried thyme
1 teaspoon curry powder
¾ teaspoon dried sage

¾ teaspoon ground allspice
½ teaspoon paprika
¼ teaspoon cayenne
¼ teaspoon salt
¼ teaspoon sugar
¼ teaspoon ground cinnamon
¼ teaspoon ground nutmeg
⅛ teaspoon ground cloves
2 teaspoons vegetable oil, preferably canola oil
1 large clove garlic, minced
1 pound large shrimp, peeled and deveined, but with tails left intact
Lemon wedges for garnish

Prepare a medium-hot barbecue fire. Oil the grill rack or coat with a nonstick vegetable spray. If using bamboo skewers, soak them at least 30 minutes in cold water.

In a small dish, combine the thyme, curry powder, sage, allspice, paprika, cayenne, salt, sugar, cinnamon, nutmeg, and cloves. Combine the oil and garlic. Brush the shrimp with the flavored oil, then sprinkle with the spice mixture to coat lightly. Let the shrimp stand 20 to 30 minutes at room temperature.

Thread the shrimp on metal or soaked bamboo skewers. Grill, turning once or twice, 3 to 5 minutes, until firm and just cooked through.

Serve the shrimp with lemon wedges.

CALORIES	63.09 KCAL	PROTEIN	9.42 GM
TOTAL FAT	2.00 GM	SATURATED FAT	.24 GM
SODIUM	136.11 MG	CHOLESTEROL	69.87 MG
CARBOHYDRATE	1.27 GM		

% calories from fat: 29.62%

GRILLED CLAMS WITH FRESH HORSERADISH SALSA

ɀ ɀ ɀ ɀ ɀ ɀ ɀ ɀ ɀ

8 to 10 servings

A covered grill is necessary here to provide enough even heat to cook the clams. You can also grill oysters in the same way, and they are just as good with this zippy salsa.

1 large ripe tomato, peeled, seeded, and finely chopped
1½ tablespoons grated fresh horseradish or 1 tablespoon prepared
  horseradish
1 tablespoon finely chopped cilantro
1 tablespoon finely chopped shallot
Salt and freshly ground black pepper
24 to 32 clams in the shell, such as littlenecks, scrubbed

In a mixing bowl, combine the tomato, horseradish, cilantro, shallot, and salt and pepper to taste. Cover and refrigerate at least 30 minutes or up to 4 hours.

Prepare a medium-hot barbecue fire in a covered grill. Oil the grill rack or coat with a nonstick vegetable spray. Grill the clams 8 to 10 minutes, until the shells open. (Discard any that do not open.)

Spoon about 1½ teaspoons salsa on each grilled clam and serve.

CALORIES	39.84 KCAL	PROTEIN	6.14 GM
TOTAL FAT	.50 GM	SATURATED FAT	.04 GM
SODIUM	27.88 MG	CHOLESTEROL	15.86 MG
CARBOHYDRATE	2.36 GM		

% calories from fat: 11.68%

GRILLED WHITE CLAM PIZZA

ι ι ι ι ι ι ι ι ι

8 to 10 appetizer or 3 to 4 main course servings

My home state of Connecticut is famous for its white clam pizzas, and Pepi's of New Haven is the granddaddy of all white clam pizzerias. Legions of locals and Yale students have lined up for years for a slice of this thin-crusted, garlicky, chopped clam 'apizza, the regional term for pizza. Lest all those Yalies who read this book write nasty notes, I disclaim any authenticity in this version. But it sure is good!

1 tablespoon extra-virgin olive oil
2 cloves garlic, minced
¼ teaspoon dried hot red pepper flakes
½ cup chopped fresh clams or 1 (6½-ounce) can chopped clams,
*   drained, with 1 tablespoon juice reserved*
⅓ cup chopped parsley, preferably flat-leaf
2 tablespoons grated Parmesan
1 tablespoon chopped fresh oregano or 1 teaspoon dried
1 (10-ounce) tube refrigerated pizza dough

Prepare a medium-hot barbecue fire. Oil the grill rack or coat with a nonstick vegetable spray. In a small bowl, combine the oil, garlic, red pepper flakes, and reserved 1 tablespoon juice from the clams. In another small bowl, combine the parsley, cheese, and oregano.

Unroll the pizza dough and place on a baking sheet. Roll or pat to a rough 12- by 14-inch rectangle. Use a sharp knife to cut into 4 equal pieces. Transfer the pizza dough from the sheet to the grill rack. Grill 3 to 4 minutes, until the crust is set and the bottom is golden brown with grill marks. Turn the dough with a spatula. Working quickly, brush with the garlic oil, then sprinkle with the clams and the parsley mixture. Grill 3 to 5 minutes more, until the bottoms of the pizzas are crisp and browned and the cheese topping is melted.

continued

Use a pizza cutter or sharp knife to cut each grilled pizza into about 6 pieces. Serve warm from a napkin-lined basket or a tray.

CALORIES	109.33 KCAL	PROTEIN	4.99 GM
TOTAL FAT	2.99 GM	SATURATED FAT	.66 GM
SODIUM	183.51 GM	CHOLESTEROL	5.15 MG
CARBOHYDRATE	15.25 GM		

% calories from fat: 24.94%

GRILLED ANTIPASTO VEGETABLES WITH ELEPHANT GARLIC AIOLI

ૅ ૅ ૅ ૅ ૅ ૅ ૅ ૅ ૅ

16 servings (about 1 ¼ cups aioli)

Elephant garlic, though big, has a mild flavor. If you use regular garlic, be sure the head is fresh and firm for the best flavor. All sorts of colorful crudités or grilled vegetables are good with this dip. It also adds a delightful fillip to plain grilled meats or fish steaks.

6 cloves elephant garlic (about 2 ounces) or 1 head regular garlic
4 teaspoons extra-virgin olive oil
⅔ cup low-fat or nonfat mayonnaise
⅓ cup low-fat or nonfat plain yogurt
2 tablespoons balsamic vinegar
¼ cup slivered fresh basil
Salt and freshly ground black pepper
16 cups assorted raw vegetables or grilled vegetables, such as broccoli
  florets, small red potatoes, carrots, or bell peppers (see note)

Prepare a medium barbecue fire.

Separate the garlic into cloves and peel them. Rub the garlic cloves with the oil, then wrap in a double thickness of aluminum foil. Grill at the edge of the coals, turning occasionally, 25 to 30 minutes, until the garlic is very soft. Mash the garlic, then stir together with the mayonnaise, yogurt, vinegar, basil, and salt and pepper to taste. Let stand at least 30 minutes or refrigerate up to 4 hours, but return to room temperature to serve.

Note: To grill broccoli, potatoes, or carrots, blanch them first in lightly salted boiling water until nearly fork tender. Rub the vegetables with oil, then grill on the rack or in a grill basket just until tender and lightly charred. Serve warm or at room temperature.

CALORIES	135.59 KCAL	PROTEIN	3.15 GM
TOTAL FAT	4.21 GM	SATURATED FAT	.87 GM
SODIUM	74.23 MG	CHOLESTEROL	3.60 MG
CARBOHYDRATE	22.16 GM		

% calories from fat: 27.23%

GRILLED CORN AND TOMATO SALSA

 ꙅ ꙅ ꙅ ꙅ ꙅ ꙅ ꙅ ꙅ ꙅ

4 servings (about 1 ½ cups)

Grilling gives a whole new dimension to salsa. I like this salsa recipe so much that I often do a few extra ears just to make the salsa. It also makes a fine relish for plain grilled chicken, steaks, or burgers.

2 ears fresh corn
1 tablespoon vegetable oil, preferably canola oil
½ teaspoon ground cumin
1 large firm and meaty tomato
2 tablespoons chopped cilantro
2 teaspoons fresh lime juice
1 to 2 teaspoons minced jalapeño
Salt and freshly ground black pepper
5-ounce box sesame melba toasts and/or bell pepper strips for dipping

Prepare a medium barbecue fire. Oil the grill rack or coat with a non-stick vegetable spray.

Peel back but do not remove the husks from the corn, and pull away and discard the silk. In a small dish, combine the oil and cumin. Rub the corn with about half of the flavored oil. Pull the husks back over the ears. Soak the corn in cold water to cover 30 minutes.

Grill, turning often, until the corn kernels are tender and the husks are well browned, about 20 minutes. About 5 minutes before the corn is done, cut the tomato into 1/2-inch slices; brush with the remaining flavored oil. Grill at the edge of the fire, turning once with a spatula, about 3 minutes, until just softened and tinged with brown.

Over a mixing bowl, cut the kernels from the cob, then scrape the cob with the blunt side of a knife to allow the corn "milk" to drip into the bowl. Coarsely chop the tomato slices and add to the bowl.

Stir in the cilantro, lime juice, jalapeño, and salt and pepper to taste. Let stand at least 15 minutes or up to 2 hours at room temperature before serving. Or refrigerate up to 8 hours, but return to room temperature for serving.

Serve surrounded by the melba toasts and/or bell pepper strips for dipping.

CALORIES	216.91 KCAL	PROTEIN	6.10 GM
TOTAL FAT	5.23 GM	SATURATED FAT	.48 GM
SODIUM	305.02 MG	CHOLESTEROL	.00 MG
CARBOHYDRATE	37.83 GM		

% calories from fat: 21.12%

GRILLED TOMATO AND BASIL PIZZAS

8 to 10 appetizer or 3 to 4 main course servings

Refrigerated pizza dough is perfect for the grill. All manner of toppings can be used following the same grilling formula, but I like the classic summertime simplicity of ripe tomatoes and basil with a sprinkling of cheese.

1 tablespoon extra-virgin olive oil
1 clove garlic, minced
¼ teaspoon dried hot red pepper flakes
1 (10-ounce) tube refrigerated pizza dough
12 ounces ripe plum tomatoes, seeded and thinly sliced
⅓ cup slivered fresh basil
½ cup (2 ounces) shredded reduced-fat mozzarella

continued

Prepare a medium-hot barbecue fire. Oil the grill rack or coat with a nonstick vegetable spray. In a small bowl, combine the oil, garlic, and red pepper flakes. Let stand 15 to 30 minutes.

Unroll the pizza dough and place on a baking sheet. Roll or pat to a rough 12- by 14-inch rectangle. Use a sharp knife to cut into 4 equal pieces. Transfer the pizza dough from the sheet to the grill rack. Grill 3 to 4 minutes, until the crust is set and the bottom is golden brown with grill marks. Turn the dough with a spatula. Working quickly, brush the garlic oil on the grilled side of the pizza dough, then arrange the tomato slices, and sprinkle with the basil and cheese. Grill 3 to 5 minutes more, until the bottoms of the pizzas are crisp and browned and the cheese topping is melted.

Use a pizza cutter or sharp knife to cut each grilled pizza into about 6 pieces. Serve warm from a napkin-lined basket.

CALORIES	115.37 KCAL	PROTEIN	5.01 GM
TOTAL FAT	3.32 GM	SATURATED FAT	.89 GM
SODIUM	191.48 MG	CHOLESTEROL	2.22 MG
CARBOHYDRATE	16.73 GM		

% calories from fat: 25.57%

GRILLED HONEY MUSTARD SWEET POTATO THINS

ι ι ι ι ι ι ι ι ι

8 appetizer servings

These crisp slices are a wonderful alternative to potato chips. In fact, some think that they are better.

2 large sweet potatoes (about 1 pound)
1 tablespoon vegetable oil, preferably canola oil
1 tablespoon honey
2 teaspoons dry white wine
2 teaspoons Dijon mustard
Salt and freshly ground black pepper

Prepare a medium barbecue fire. Oil the grill rack or coat with a non-stick vegetable spray.

Peel the sweet potatoes and cut lengthwise into slices about ⅛ inch thick. Rub with the vegetable oil. Grill, turning occasionally, until the sweet potatoes are lightly golden, about 8 minutes.

In a small bowl, combine the honey, wine, and mustard. Brush over the sweet potato slices and continue to grill until rich golden brown and crisp, about 3 to 5 minutes more.

Season with salt and pepper and serve in a napkin-lined basket.

CALORIES	68.33 KCAL	PROTEIN	.67 GM
TOTAL FAT	1.90 GM	SATURATED FAT	.14 GM
SODIUM	43.02 MG	CHOLESTEROL	.00 MG
CARBOHYDRATE	12.26 GM		

% calories from fat: 24.84%

GRILLED POTATO "CHIPS"

4 to 6 servings

Malt vinegar is the traditional condiment for "chips" in England. It is just as good here! These crispy potato slices are also delicious plain or with a dollop of low-fat or no-fat sour cream mixed with some chopped fresh chives.

2 large Idaho baking potatoes (about 1 pound total)
1 tablespoon vegetable oil, preferably canola oil
Salt and freshly ground black pepper
2 teaspoons malt vinegar

Prepare a medium-hot barbecue fire. Oil the grill rack or coat with a nonstick vegetable spray.

Cut the unpeeled potatoes into lengthwise slices slightly less than ¼ inch thick. Rub with the oil.

Grill the potato slices, turning occasionally, until rich golden brown and crisp on the outside and tender in the interior, 10 to 13 minutes total. Sprinkle with salt and pepper and the vinegar and serve warm from a napkin-lined basket.

CALORIES	91.32 KCAL	PROTEIN	1.98 GM
TOTAL FAT	2.81 GM	SATURATED FAT	.21 GM
SODIUM	6.37 MG	CHOLESTEROL	.00 MG
CARBOHYDRATE	15.18 GM		

% calories from fat: 26.92%

GRILLED CAPONATA CROSTINI

ι ι ι ι ι ι ι ι ι

12 to 14 servings (about 2½ cups caponata)

This grilled variation on a favorite Sicilian sweet-and-sour eggplant dish is one of my most-often-served summertime cocktail party canapés. Both the crostini and the vegetables should be grilled in advance, so that only the easy assembly is left to the last minute. Or you can serve the caponata in a bowl surrounded by the toasts and let your guests make their own. Caponata is also excellent for supper when tossed with about 1 pound cooked spaghetti.

1 medium eggplant (about 12 ounces)
Salt
1 medium sweet onion, such as Vidalia
2 tablespoons extra-virgin olive oil
1 rib celery
1 large ripe tomato, peeled, seeded, and chopped (about 8 ounces)
2 tablespoons balsamic or red wine vinegar
2 tablespoons raisins
2 teaspoons sugar
¼ teaspoon dried hot red pepper flakes
⅓ cup chopped parsley, preferably flat-leaf
¼ cup chopped Sicilian or other Mediterranean olives
2 teaspoons drained small capers
1 long loaf Italian bread (about 16 ounces)

Cut the unpeeled eggplant lengthwise into slices ½ inch thick. Sprinkle both sides of each slice with salt and let drain in a colander 30 minutes. Rinse well in cold water and pat dry on paper towels.

Prepare a medium barbecue fire. Oil the grill rack or coat with a nonstick vegetable spray.

continued

Cut the onion into slices slightly less than ½ inch thick. Rub the eggplant slices and onion with 1 tablespoon of the oil. Grill, turning occasionally, until the eggplant and onion are soft and lightly charred, 12 to 15 minutes. Let the vegetables cool, then coarsely chop.

In a large skillet, heat the remaining 1 tablespoon oil. Sauté the celery over medium-low heat about 5 minutes, until beginning to soften. Add the grilled vegetables, tomato, vinegar, raisins, sugar, and red pepper flakes. Simmer over medium-low heat, stirring often, 10 minutes. Stir in the parsley, olives, and capers and simmer 5 minutes, until very thick. (If the mixture seems too thick and likely to burn, add a small amount of water.) Let the caponata cool. (This can be prepared early in the day or even a day ahead and refrigerated, but return to room temperature to serve.)

Cut the bread crosswise into slices ½ inch thick. Grill the bread slices, turning once, about 1 minute to lightly toast both sides. (Crostini can be toasted early in the day and reserved at room temperature.)

Spoon the caponata onto the crostini and serve at room temperature.

CALORIES	146.72 KCAL	PROTEIN	3.87 GM
TOTAL FAT	4.43 GM	SATURATED FAT	.70 GM
SODIUM	334.74 MG	CHOLESTEROL	.00 MG
CARBOHYDRATE	23.48 GM		

% calories from fat: 26.70%

CURRIED GRILLED VEGETABLES

6 servings

Cauliflower, carrots, and potatoes are common ingredients in Indian dishes. When marinated in curried yogurt, skewered, and grilled, they make great nibbles with drinks, zippy side dishes for simple grilled meats or chicken, or even a main course. To save time, buy packaged cauliflower florets and baby carrots at the supermarket.

1 pound red potatoes, cut in 1½-inch chunks
8 ounces baby carrots or slim carrots, cut in 1½-inch lengths
3 cups cauliflower florets
1½ cups low-fat or nonfat plain yogurt
2 cloves garlic, minced
1½ teaspoons curry powder
½ teaspoon ground cumin
½ teaspoon salt
¼ teaspoon freshly ground black pepper
⅛ teaspoon cayenne
¼ cup chopped cilantro

Cook the potatoes in a large pot of lightly salted boiling water 3 minutes. Add the carrots and cook 2 minutes. Add the cauliflower and cook an additional 3 minutes, until all vegetables are barely fork tender. Drain well on paper towels. (The vegetables can be parboiled several hours ahead and kept at room temperature.)

Prepare a medium barbecue fire. Oil the grill rack or coat with a nonstick vegetable spray. If using bamboo skewers, soak them in cold water to cover at least 30 minutes.

In a mixing bowl, combine the yogurt, garlic, curry powder,

continued

cumin, salt, pepper, and cayenne. Place the vegetables in a shallow dish and pour ¾ cup of the seasoned yogurt over them. Stir to coat the vegetables and let stand 15 minutes or up to one hour.

Thread the vegetables onto metal or soaked bamboo skewers. Grill, turning occasionally, 6 to 8 minutes, until tender and lightly browned.

Stir the cilantro into the remaining seasoned yogurt and serve as a dipping sauce for the vegetables.

CALORIES	129.38 KCAL	PROTEIN	5.94 GM
TOTAL FAT	1.27 GM	SATURATED FAT	.58 GM
SODIUM	339.50 MG	CHOLESTEROL	3.40 MG
CARBOHYDRATE	24.64 GM		

% calories from fat: 8.54%

SEAFOOD

Although serious fishermen everywhere have long known the merits of seafood cooked on the grill, it is only lately that home cooks have been privy to the savory secret. Just in the nick of time, too. Now that we know about the low-fat protein provided by most fish and shellfish, and have learned how to use it to its best advantage on the grill, a whole new world of healthy possibilities has opened up.

Fish cookery in general has seemed daunting in the past mainly because of a lack of knowledge and a confusion about fish nomenclature. Similar varieties go by different names depending upon where they are caught and sold. And until recently, the middle of the country rarely saw much in the way of saltwater seafood, save for shrimp and maybe some frozen sole. Now, with the increased demand, all manner of fresh fish is readily available almost everywhere.

But for grilling, the field narrows. Firm-fleshed fish, especially such fish steaks as swordfish, tuna, salmon, or halibut, and such fillets as snapper, grouper, or monkfish, as well as whole small fish like trout, hold up best to grilling. Very delicate fish fillets like sole or flounder will fall apart on the grill rack. Most shellfish are delicious when grilled, but such small ones as shrimp and scallops are easiest to grill on skewers. Clams and lobster, rarely thought of as grill fare, are really terrific enhanced by the slight smokiness of an open fire.

Overcooking and subsequent drying out are the main problems in outdoor fish cookery. In general, the trusted Canadian cooking rule of 10 minutes per inch of thickness applies to grilling, but since outdoor cooking is variable and a minute or so each way makes a big difference to seafood, test a little early. Seafood is done when it is opaque throughout.

THAI-STYLE GRILLED SEA BASS SOUP

∼ ∼ ∼ ∼ ∼ ∼ ∼ ∼ ∼

6 servings

This is a sort of Asian gumbo. Delicate sea bass is wonderful here, but
you could use almost any fish and/or shellfish combination, such as
tuna and scallops or shrimp, or even shellfish only. A plus for entertaining is that the soup base can be made a day ahead, leaving only the
grilling for the last minute.

1½ tablespoons vegetable oil, preferably canola oil
1 large onion, chopped
1 small green bell pepper, thinly sliced
1 small yellow bell pepper, thinly sliced
2 large cloves garlic, minced
2 jalapeño or Scotch bonnet peppers, minced
2 teaspoons curry powder
2 cups diced plum tomatoes or 1 (14½- to 16-ounce) can diced tomatoes
2 cups bottled clam juice
¼ cup fresh lime juice
3 tablespoons Thai fish sauce (nam pla)
Freshly ground black pepper
1½ pounds sea bass fillets
Salt
½ cup chopped cilantro
3 cups hot cooked white rice

In a large saucepan, heat 1 tablespoon of the oil. Stir in the onion, bell
peppers, and garlic. Cover the saucepan and cook over medium-low
heat, stirring occasionally, about 8 minutes, until vegetables are softened. Stir in the jalapeños and curry powder and cook, uncovered, 30

seconds. Add the tomatoes with juices, clam juice, lime juice, fish sauce, and ½ cup water. Simmer, covered, 6 minutes. Taste and season with pepper. (The soup base can be made a day ahead and refrigerated. Reheat before continuing.)

Prepare a medium-hot barbecue fire. Oil the grill rack or coat with a nonstick vegetable spray.

Rub the fish with the remaining ½ tablespoon of oil and season lightly with salt and pepper. Grill the fish, turning once carefully with a spatula, about 8 minutes, until just cooked through.

Use a ½-cup measure to spoon the rice into each of 6 shallow soup bowls. Use a spatula to transfer the fish fillets next to the rice. Stir the cilantro into the soup, then ladle over the fish and rice.

CALORIES	333.70 KCAL	PROTEIN	26.63 GM
TOTAL FAT	7.20 GM	SATURATED FAT	1.12 GM
SODIUM	261.06 MG	CHOLESTEROL	46.53 MG
CARBOHYDRATE	39.41 GM		

% calories from fat: 19.69%

Grilled Mahimahi with Pineapple and Pepper Salsa

8 servings

If you can't find a really flavorful ripe pineapple, use canned crushed pineapple in juice. Grouper and monkfish are also good choices for this tropical treatment.

1½ cups chopped fresh pineapple or 1 (12- to 16-ounce) can crushed
* pineapple in juice*
1 small red bell pepper, coarsely chopped
½ cup chopped scallion
1 or 2 jalapeños, minced
3 tablespoons chopped cilantro
1 tablespoon fresh lime juice
½ teaspoon salt
2 pounds mahimahi fillets
1 tablespoon vegetable oil, preferably canola oil
¼ teaspoon cayenne
Cilantro sprigs for garnish

In a medium bowl, stir together the pineapple, bell pepper, scallion, jalapeños, cilantro, lime juice, and ¼ teaspoon of the salt. Reserve at room temperature up to 1 hour or refrigerate up to 8 hours, but return to room temperature to serve.

Prepare a medium-hot barbecue fire. Oil the grill rack or coat with a nonstick vegetable spray. Rub the fish with the oil, then sprinkle with the remaining ¼ teaspoon salt and the cayenne. Grill, turning once, about 10 minutes total, until just cooked through.

Serve the fish with some of the salsa spooned over and garnished with cilantro sprigs.

CALORIES	131.41 KCAL	PROTEIN	21.32 GM
TOTAL FAT	2.63 GM	SATURATED FAT	.33 GM
SODIUM	238.62 MG	CHOLESTEROL	82.85 MG
CARBOHYDRATE	4.91 GM		

% calories from fat: 18.40%

GRILLED RED SNAPPER WITH TOMATILLO SALSA

6 servings

Fresh tomatillos are increasingly available across the country, and their tart lemony flavor makes a wonderful piquant salsa. If you substitute canned tomatillos, don't cook them.

12 ounces fresh tomatillos or 1 (12- to 16-ounce) can, drained
½ cup finely chopped onion
2 cloves garlic, minced
1 to 2 jalapeños, minced
⅓ cup chopped cilantro
½ teaspoon salt
1½ pounds red snapper fillets
1 tablespoon vegetable oil, preferably canola oil
1 teaspoon chili powder
Cilantro sprigs for garnish

continued

Remove the papery brown husks from fresh tomatillos. Simmer them in water to cover 2 to 3 minutes, until they are just tender. Drain and cool, then chop the tomatillos. If using canned tomatillos, simply chop them.

In a mixing bowl, combine the tomatillos, onion, garlic, jalapeños, cilantro, and salt. Let stand at least 15 minutes or refrigerate up to 4 hours, but return to room temperature to serve.

Prepare a medium-hot barbecue fire. Oil the grill rack or coat with a nonstick vegetable spray. Rub the fish with the oil, then sprinkle with the chili powder. Grill the fish, turning once carefully with a spatula, about 8 minutes, until just cooked through.

Serve the fish with the salsa and garnish with the cilantro sprigs.

CALORIES	156.56 KCAL	PROTEIN	24.37 GM
TOTAL FAT	4.13 GM	SATURATED FAT	.48 GM
SODIUM	260.21 MG	CHOLESTEROL	41.99 MG
CARBOHYDRATE	4.33 GM		

% calories from fat: 24.45%

GRILLED GROUPER WITH MULTI-MELON SALSA

ↄ ↄ ↄ ↄ ↄ ↄ ↄ ↄ ↄ

6 servings

Because cut-up melon is readily available at supermarket salad bars, you can use several kinds for a more colorful salsa. The only variety to avoid is watermelon.

1 cup diced mixed melons, such as cantaloupe, honeydew, and
  Cranshaw
⅓ cup chopped red onion
¼ cup chopped mint
3 tablespoons fresh lime juice
1 tablespoon honey
¼ teaspoon Tabasco sauce or to taste
½ teaspoon salt
1½ pounds grouper fillets
2 teaspoons vegetable oil, preferably canola oil
¼ teaspoon freshly ground black pepper
Small mint sprigs for garnish

In a small bowl, stir together the melon, onion, mint, lime juice,
honey, Tabasco sauce, and ¼ teaspoon of the salt. Reserve at room
temperature for up to 1 hour or refrigerate up to 8 hours, but return
to room temperature to serve.

Prepare a medium-hot barbecue fire. Oil the grill rack or coat
with a nonstick vegetable spray. Rub the fish with the oil, then sprinkle with the remaining ¼ teaspoon salt and the pepper. Grill, turning
once, about 10 minutes, until just cooked through.

Serve the fish with the salsa spooned over and garnished with the
mint sprigs.

CALORIES	144.03 KCAL	PROTEIN	22.34 GM
TOTAL FAT	2.73 GM	SATURATED FAT	.36 GM
SODIUM	248.78 MG	CHOLESTEROL	41.99 MG
CARBOHYDRATE	6.76 GM		

% calories from fat: 17.42%

GRILLED TUNA NIÇOISE

ε ε ε ε ε ε ε ε ε

4 servings

A variation of the classic meal-size salad from the south of France, the grilled version is especially flavorful, and far lower in fat than the original. A slim baguette and a glass of good wine make this a special dinner for a warm summer evening. Don't be put off by the long ingredient list; this is a breeze to prepare.

1 pound small red potatoes
1 pound green string beans, trimmed
3 tablespoons reduced-sodium chicken broth
2 tablespoons balsamic vinegar
2 tablespoons extra-virgin olive oil
1 large clove garlic, minced
2 teaspoons chopped fresh rosemary or ½ teaspoon dried
¼ teaspoon salt
¼ teaspoon freshly ground black pepper
1 pound tuna steak, cut about ¾ inch thick
6 diagonal slices French bread (baguette)
1 head red-leaf lettuce, separated into leaves
1 tablespoon small capers, drained
2 tablespoons chopped parsley
1 tomato, cut in 8 wedges
8 Niçoise olives

If the potatoes are larger than 1½ inches in diameter, cut them in half. Cook the potatoes in boiling salted water about 7 minutes, until barely tender. Add the beans to the potatoes and cook 2 to 3 minutes, until the beans are crisp-tender and the potatoes are cooked. Drain the vegetables in a strainer and rinse under cold water to stop the cooking and set the color. (The vegetables can be cooked early in the day and reserved at room temperature.)

In a small bowl, whisk together the broth, vinegar, oil, garlic, rosemary, salt, and pepper. Lightly brush the tuna with about 2 teaspoons of the vinaigrette. Let stand about 30 minutes.

Prepare a medium-hot barbecue fire. Oil the grill rack or coat with a nonstick vegetable spray.

Thread the potatoes onto metal skewers. Brush with about 2 teaspoons of the vinaigrette. Grill the tuna and the potatoes, turning once, about 8 minutes, until the fish is just cooked through and the potatoes are browned. Grill the bread about 30 seconds per side, until lightly toasted.

Make a bed of lettuce leaves on a platter or 4 serving plates. Cut the tuna into 1-inch chunks. Arrange the tuna, potatoes, and beans in separate areas on the lettuce. Sprinkle the fish with the capers. Garnish with parsley-sprinkled tomato wedges and the olives. Drizzle the remaining vinaigrette over the entire salad. Garnish with the grilled bread.

CALORIES	319.42 KCAL	PROTEIN	23.33 GM
TOTAL FAT	10.07 GM	SATURATED FAT	1.87 GM
SODIUM	388.31 MG	CHOLESTEROL	28.75 MG
CARBOHYDRATE	34.47 GM		

% calories from fat: 28.16%

GRILLED TUNA AND CUCUMBER SALAD WITH WASABI VINAIGRETTE

~ ~ ~ ~ ~ ~ ~ ~ ~

6 servings

I must confess that, although I love both seafood and Japanese food, the sushi craze passed me by. I liked all the accoutrements and the lightness of the concept, but I could never quite warm up to raw fish. Here, many of the classic sushi flavors complement grilled tuna, and you could use shark or swordfish with equal success. Mirin, wasabi powder, and Thai fish sauce are available at Asian markets, as well as in many large supermarkets.

3 tablespoons reduced-sodium soy sauce
2 tablespoons mirin or dry sherry
1½ tablespoons fresh lime juice
1 tablespoon wasabi paste (see note)
*2 teaspoons Thai fish sauce (*nam pla*)*
1 teaspoon rice wine vinegar
1 tablespoon sesame oil
1 pound tuna steak, cut about ¾ inch thick
1 large seedless cucumber, thinly sliced
⅓ cup thinly sliced scallions
6 toasted rice cakes

Prepare a medium-hot barbecue fire. Oil the grill rack or coat with a nonstick vegetable spray.

In a small bowl, whisk together the soy sauce, mirin, lime juice, wasabi paste, fish sauce, vinegar, and 2 teaspoons of the oil. Use the remaining teaspoon of oil to rub on all sides of the fish.

Grill the fish, turning once, about 8 minutes, until just cooked through. Use a sharp knife to slice the fish about ½ inch thick.

Make a bed of cucumbers on a platter or 6 plates. Arrange the fish on the cucumbers and drizzle with the vinaigrette. Sprinkle the salad with the scallions. Garnish with the rice cakes.

Note: Reconstitute wasabi powder according to package directions to make 2 teaspoons paste.

CALORIES	228.89 KCAL	PROTEIN	20.97 GM
TOTAL FAT	6.97 GM	SATURATED FAT	1.48 GM
SODIUM	484.35 MG	CHOLESTEROL	28.75 MG
CARBOHYDRATE	18.00 GM		

% calories from fat: 28.69%

GRILLED SALMON WITH DILLED CUCUMBER YOGURT SAUCE

12 servings

A "side," or whole fillet, of salmon makes a lovely presentation for a party buffet, but can be tricky to maneuver on the grill if you don't have a couple of wide spatulas. If you wish, have the salmon cut into 5 or 6 pieces for grilling, then cut each in half for serving. In either case, for the prettiest look, arrange the grilled fish on a generous bed of fresh dill and garnish with thinly sliced lemon and cucumbers on small mounds of cold parsleyed rice. If your cucumbers are garden fresh or the seedless variety, you won't have to peel them. Incidentally, the sauce makes a good crudité dip or dressing for potato salad.

continued

DILL AND CUCUMBER YOGURT SAUCE

¾ cup nonfat or low-fat plain yogurt
⅓ cup nonfat or low-fat mayonnaise
½ cup coarsely seeded and coarsely chopped cucumber
¼ cup chopped fresh dill
1 teaspoon grated lemon zest
Salt and freshly ground black pepper

SALMON

1 whole salmon fillet (2½ to 3 pounds)
2 teaspoons vegetable oil, preferably canola oil
1 teaspoon coarsely ground black pepper
1 bunch dill
6 cups cooked and chilled rice tossed with ½ cup chopped parsley
1 lemon, thinly sliced
1 cucumber, thinly sliced

To make the sauce, stir together all the ingredients in a medium bowl. Let stand 15 minutes at room temperature or refrigerate at least 1 hour or up to 4 hours before serving.

To prepare the salmon, make a barbecue fire. Use tongs to push the coals to one side for indirect cooking. Oil the grill rack or coat with a nonstick vegetable spray.

Rub the fish with the oil, sprinkle with pepper, then place, skin side up, on the grill rack on the side away from the coals. Grill about 7 minutes, then use a large spatula to carefully loosen the fish from the grill. Use two large spatulas to turn the fish skin side down. Grill another 7 minutes or until the fish is just cooked through.

While the fish is grilling, on a large oval or rectangular platter make a bed of the dill. Use 2 spatulas to carefully loosen, then remove, the fish from the grill and set it on the bed of dill. Make 12 mounds of the parsleyed rice around the fish. Garnish the platter with

the lemon and cucumber slices. Spoon a little of the sauce onto the
fish and serve the remainder on the side.

CALORIES	306.68 KCAL	PROTEIN	24.53 GM
TOTAL FAT	7.70 GM	SATURATED FAT	1.16 GM
SODIUM	144.07 MG	CHOLESTEROL	57.50 MG
CARBOHYDRATE	33.06 GM		

% calories from fat: 23.12%

GRILLED SALMON AND WATERCRESS SALAD
WITH GINGER VINAIGRETTE

₹ ₹ ₹ ₹ ₹ ₹ ₹ ₹ ₹

6 servings

The deep green color and bitter flavor of watercress make it the perfect base for this salad, with its light and spicy dressing. Pink salmon
looks particularly nice on the rice, but swordfish will taste terrific too.

¼ cup reduced-sodium chicken broth or vegetable broth
3 tablespoons fresh lime juice
3 tablespoons grated fresh ginger
2 tablespoons finely chopped shallots
1 tablespoon honey
1 tablespoon reduced-sodium soy sauce
1 clove garlic, minced
1 ½ tablespoons vegetable oil, preferably canola oil
1 pound skinless salmon fillets
Salt and freshly ground black pepper
2 small bunches watercress sprigs

continued

1 teaspoon grated lime zest
3 cups cooked and cooled rice

In a small bowl, whisk together the broth, lime juice, ginger, shallots, honey, soy sauce, garlic, and 1 tablespoon of the oil. Reserve at room temperature up to 4 hours or refrigerate up to 12 hours, but return to room temperature to serve.

Prepare a medium-hot barbecue fire. Oil the grill rack or coat with a nonstick vegetable spray. Rub the fish with the remaining ½ tablespoon oil, then season lightly with salt and pepper. Grill the fish, turning once, 8 to 10 minutes, until just cooked through.

To serve, toss the watercress with half of the vinaigrette, then spread out on 4 serving plates. Stir the lime zest into the rice. Spoon the rice in the center of the watercress. Cut the fish into ½-inch strips and arrange on the watercress surrounding the rice. Drizzle the rice and fish with the remaining vinaigrette.

CALORIES	294.00 KCAL	PROTEIN	19.04 GM
TOTAL FAT	8.57 GM	SATURATED FAT	1.07 GM
SODIUM	179.73 MG	CHOLESTEROL	41.61 MG
CARBOHYDRATE	33.96 GM		

% calories from fat: 26.67%

GRILLED SHARK STEAKS WITH BLACK BEAN AND MANGO SALSA

6 servings

Shark, despite its scary connotation, is a rather mild-tasting fish and a relatively inexpensive alternative to swordfish. It is also quite delicious with this tangy, hot/sweet salsa.

2 *ripe mangoes, peeled and coarsely diced*
1 *cup soaked, cooked, and drained black beans or drained and rinsed*
  canned black beans
⅔ *cup chopped scallions, including green tops*
¼ *cup chopped cilantro*
1 *tablespoon seeded, chopped jalapeño*
1 *tablespoon honey*
5 *tablespoons fresh lime juice*
4 *teaspoons vegetable oil, preferably canola oil*
¾ *teaspoon ground cumin*
½ *teaspoon salt*
1½ *pounds shark steak, cut about ¾ inch thick*

In a mixing bowl, stir together the mangoes, beans, scallions, cilantro, jalapeño, honey, 4 tablespoons of the lime juice, 2 teaspoons of the oil, ½ teaspoon of the cumin, and ¼ teaspoon of the salt. Let stand 30 minutes at room temperature or refrigerate up to 4 hours, but return to room temperature for serving.

Rub the fish with the remaining 2 teaspoons of the oil; sprinkle with the remaining lime juice, cumin, and salt. Let stand 15 to 30 minutes.

Prepare a medium-hot barbecue fire. Oil the grill rack or coat with a nonstick vegetable spray. Grill the fish, turning once, about 8 minutes, until just cooked through.

Serve the fish accompanied by the salsa.

CALORIES	259.98 KCAL	PROTEIN	24.47 GM
TOTAL FAT	8.02 GM	SATURATED FAT	1.23 GM
SODIUM	268.72 MG	CHOLESTEROL	51.71 MG
CARBOHYDRATE	23.35 GM		

% calories from fat: 27.39%

GRILLED SOFT-SHELL CRABS WITH TOMATO TARTARE SAUCE

? ? ? ? ? ? ? ? ?

6 servings

Totally edible soft-shell crabs, a spring and summer tradition in the Chesapeake Bay area, are now often shipped to other parts of the country. The fishmonger will clean the live crabs when you buy them, since they deteriorate rather quickly once killed. However, when crabs are unavailable or out of season, I have used commercially frozen ones with some success.

¼ cup nonfat mayonnaise
¼ cup nonfat plain yogurt
3 tablespoons pickle relish
2 tablespoons fresh lemon juice
2 tablespoons chopped parsley
1 tablespoon tomato paste
2 teaspoons Dijon mustard
12 fresh soft-shell crabs, cleaned
1½ tablespoons vegetable oil, preferably canola oil
1 teaspoon Old Bay Seasoning or other seafood seasoning blend
12 slices white bread toast
Shredded iceberg lettuce

Prepare a medium-hot barbecue fire. Oil the grill rack or coat with a nonstick vegetable spray. In a small dish, blend together the mayonnaise, yogurt, relish, lemon juice, parsley, tomato paste, and mustard. Rub the crabs with the oil, then sprinkle with the Old Bay Seasoning.

Grill the crabs, back side down, 3 to 5 minutes, until lightly browned. Turn and grill on the other side about 3 to 5 minutes more, until lightly browned and cooked through.

Spread one side of the toasts with the flavored mayonnaise sauce. Make sandwiches with the crabs and shredded lettuce.

CALORIES	386.82 KCAL	PROTEIN	39.31 GM
TOTAL FAT	11.15 GM	SATURATED FAT	1.71 GM
SODIUM	1,050.14 MG	CHOLESTEROL	174.08
CARBOHYDRATE	30.02 GM		

% calories from fat: 26.57%

GRILLED SEA SCALLOPS AND GRAPEFRUIT

ι ι ι ι ι ι ι ι ι

4 servings

Scallops and grapefruit are wonderful together, and when grilled with the anise flavor of Pernod and tarragon they make a delightful main course for a light summery meal. Be sure to use sea scallops, rather than the very tiny bay scallops. Cut any especially large ones ones into rough 1- to 1½-inch chunks for even grilling.

¼ cup fresh grapefruit juice
2 tablespoons Pernod
1 tablespoon chopped fresh tarragon or 1 teaspoon dried
2 teaspoons vegetable oil, preferably canola oil
¼ teaspoon salt
¼ teaspoon freshly ground black pepper
1 pound sea scallops
2 small grapefruits, peeled and sectioned
8 scallions, trimmed to leave 2 inches of green part
2 cups cooked white rice
Tarragon sprigs for garnish, optional

continued

In a shallow dish, combine the grapefruit juice, Pernod, tarragon, oil, salt, and pepper. Add the scallops, grapefruit, and scallions, stirring to coat with the marinade. Let stand 30 minutes.

Prepare a medium barbecue fire. Oil the grill rack or coat with a nonstick vegetable spray. Alternately thread the scallops, grapefruit, and scallions onto metal skewers. Grill, turning occasionally and brushing with the marinade, about 5 minutes, until tinged with brown and the scallops are cooked through.

Spoon the rice onto a platter, then arrange the scallops, grapefruit, and scallions on the rice. Garnish with tarragon sprigs, if desired.

CALORIES	318.64 KCAL	PROTEIN	23.07 GM
TOTAL FAT	3.58 GM	SATURATED FAT	.33 GM
SODIUM	325.09 MG	CHOLESTEROL	37.45 MG
CARBOHYDRATE	44.65 GM		

% calories from fat: 10.63%

GRILLED SCALLOPS ESCABECHE

ι ι ι ι ι ι ι ι ι

4 servings

Pescado Escabeche is a traditional Spanish dish in which sautéed seafood is marinated in a spicy pickling liquid. This simple version uses only a few herbs and spices, but packs a wonderful flavor punch. Shrimp or swordfish chunks are good substitutes for the scallops. Make this a couple of hours ahead so that the flavors mingle before serving.

¼ cup white wine vinegar
¼ cup dry sherry
10 whole allspice berries
2 teaspoons chopped fresh thyme
4 thin slices fresh gingerroot
1 to 2 jalapeños, seeded and chopped
1 large clove garlic, slivered
½ teaspoon salt
1½ tablespoons extra-virgin olive oil
1 pound sea scallops
1 sweet onion, such as Vidalia or Maui, cut horizontally into
    ¼- inch slices
1 red bell pepper, quartered

Prepare a medium-hot barbecue fire. Oil the grill rack or coat with a nonstick vegetable spray.

In a shallow dish, combine the vinegar, sherry, allspice, thyme, gingerroot, jalapeños, garlic, salt, and ½ tablespoon of the oil. Rub the scallops, onion slices, and pepper quarters with the remaining 1 tablespoon of the oil. Thread the scallops onto metal skewers.

Grill the onions and peppers, turning once or twice, 8 to 10 minutes, until softened and lightly charred. Grill the scallops, turning once or twice, 6 to 8 minutes, until lightly browned and just cooked through. Thinly slice the grilled peppers and separate the onion into rings. Add the onion, peppers, and scallops to the marinade. Stir to coat. Let stand about 30 minutes at room temperature or refrigerate up to 3 hours, but return to room temperature to serve.

CALORIES	204.11 KCAL	PROTEIN	20.34 GM
TOTAL FAT	6.25 GM	SATURATED FAT	.84 GM
SODIUM	464.96 MG	CHOLESTEROL	37.45 MG
CARBOHYDRATE	12.78 GM		

% calories from fat: 29.80%

SWORDFISH TACOS

ι   ι   ι   ι   ι   ι   ι   ι   ι

8 servings

Shrimp also makes a fine taco, as does halibut or salmon. The Grilled
Corn and Tomato Salsa can be made ahead of time.

1 pound swordfish steaks, cut about ¾ inch thick
2 teaspoons vegetable oil, preferably canola oil
1 tablespoon chili powder
6 corn or flour tortillas
1½ cups Grilled Corn and Tomato Salsa (page 28) or purchased
  chunky salsa
2 cups shredded iceberg lettuce
⅓ cup low-fat or nonfat yogurt or nonfat sour cream

For the tacos, prepare a medium-hot fire. Oil the grill rack or coat
with a nonstick vegetable spray. Rub the swordfish with the oil, then
sprinkle with the chili powder. Wrap the tortillas in foil.

Grill the fish, turning once, about 8 minutes, until the fish is just
cooked through. Grill the foil-wrapped tortilla package about 3 minutes, at the edge of the fire, until heated. Cut the fish into thin slices
or rough ¾-inch chunks. Mix with about two-thirds of the salsa and
spoon into the tortillas. Sprinkle with the lettuce and fold over to
make a soft taco shape. Serve garnished with the yogurt and the
remaining salsa.

CALORIES	247.35 KCAL	PROTEIN	15.06 GM
TOTAL FAT	8.53 GM	SATURATED FAT	1.24 GM
SODIUM	237.98 MG	CHOLESTEROL	19.87 MG
CARBOHYDRATE	28.20 GM		

% calories from fat: 29.73%

Skewered Cajun Shrimp and Okra

≀ ≀ ≀ ≀ ≀ ≀ ≀ ≀ ≀

4 servings

This is a recipe for those who really like pepper and spices. To tame the heat, serve the shrimp and okra over steamed rice seasoned with lemon zest and juice.

1 tablespoon paprika
1 tablespoon chili powder
½ teaspoon ground cumin
½ teaspoon salt
½ teaspoon cayenne
1 tablespoon grated onion
1 clove garlic, minced
4 tablespoons fresh lemon juice
1 cup plus 3 tablespoons bottled clam juice
2 teaspoons extra-virgin olive oil
1 pound large or jumbo shrimp, peeled and deveined
8 ounces okra (about 2 cups)
1 cup white rice
Salt
2 teaspoons grated lemon zest

Combine the paprika, chili powder, cumin, salt, and cayenne. (This can be mixed several days in advance and stored in a tightly covered container.)

In a shallow dish, combine the spice mix with the onion, garlic, 3 tablespoons of the lemon juice, 3 tablespoons of the clam juice, and the oil. Add the shrimp and okra, turning to coat. Let stand 30 minutes.

Prepare a medium-hot barbecue fire. Oil the grill rack or coat with a nonstick vegetable spray.

continued

To cook the rice, bring the remaining 1 cup of clam juice, 1 tablespoon lemon juice, and 1 cup water to a boil. Add a pinch of salt and stir in the rice. Cover the pot and simmer over medium-low heat about 20 minutes, until the liquid is absorbed and the rice is tender. Stir in the lemon zest.

Thread the shrimp and okra on separate metal skewers. Grill the okra, turning occasionally, 6 to 8 minutes, until tender and lightly charred. Grill the shrimp, turning once or twice, about 3 to 5 minutes, until opaque and just cooked through.

Serve the shrimp and okra over the rice.

CALORIES	328.57 KCAL	PROTEIN	24.07 GM
TOTAL FAT	4.85 GM	SATURATED FAT	.72 GM
SODIUM	593.12 MG	CHOLESTEROL	139.74 MG
CARBOHYDRATE	46.23 GM		

% calories from fat: 13.43%

GRILLED SHRIMP, ORANGE, AND FENNEL SALAD

6 servings

This sophisticated salad makes an especially dramatic presentation with jumbo shrimp, but large shrimp will taste just as good, though they must be skewered for cooking. I've also used large sea scallops with great success. Don't core the fennel bulb until after grilling, so that the wedges will hold together.

1 small fennel bulb (about 10 ounces)
1 pound jumbo shrimp (about 12 to 16), peeled and deveined
2 seedless oranges, peeled and cut into slices slightly less than
  ½ inch thick

2 tablespoons extra-virgin olive oil
1½ tablespoons fresh orange juice
1½ tablespoons fresh lemon juice
1 teaspoon grated orange zest
1 teaspoon grated lemon zest
½ teaspoon freshly ground black pepper
¼ teaspoon salt
6 slices Italian bread
6 cups torn baby lettuces
2 tablespoons crumbled feta

Trim the fennel bulb, but do not core. Cut it into 8 wedges. Rub the fennel, shrimp, and orange slices with 1 tablespoon of the oil.

To make the dressing, whisk together the remaining 1 tablespoon oil, the orange and lemon juices, orange and lemon zests, pepper, and salt.

Prepare a medium-hot barbecue fire. Oil the grill rack or coat with a nonstick vegetable spray.

Grill the fennel, turning several times, about 12 minutes, until crisp-tender and browned. Grill the shrimp, turning once, about 10 minutes, until just cooked through. Grill the orange slices about 6 minutes, turning once, until softened and tinged with brown. Grill the bread about 30 seconds per side until lightly toasted.

To serve, toss the lettuces with about three quarters of the dressing and place on serving plates. Cut the core from the fennel, then separate the wedges into sections. Arrange the shrimp and oranges on the lettuces, scatter the fennel over, and sprinkle with the cheese. Drizzle with the remaining vinaigrette. Garnish with the grilled bread.

CALORIES	239.89 KCAL	PROTEIN	17.27 GM
TOTAL FAT	7.73 GM	SATURATED FAT	1.56 GM
SODIUM	432.69 MG	CHOLESTEROL	95.66 MG
CARBOHYDRATE	26.00 GM		

% calories from fat: 28.67%

GRILLED LEMON AND LICORICE LOBSTER

~ ~ ~ ~ ~ ~ ~ ~ ~

4 servings

This is a terrific way to enjoy lobster, and the potatoes and corn turn the meal into a real New England shore dinner. Splitting a live lobster isn't hard to do, but if you are squeamish about it, first plunge it into boiling water for a couple of minutes, then split. If you dislike the whole job, ask the fishmonger to do it no more than a couple of hours before you plan to cook. A covered grill is necessary for cooking lobsters.

4 tablespoons bottled clam juice
3 tablespoons fresh lemon juice
3 tablespoons chopped shallots
1 tablespoon minced fresh tarragon or 1 teaspoon dried
1½ teaspoons Dijon mustard
1½ teaspoons Pernod
¼ teaspoon salt
¼ teaspoon freshly ground black pepper
2½ tablespoons extra-virgin olive oil
4 live lobsters (each about 1¼ pounds)
Lemon wedges for garnish
Tarragon sprigs for garnish
4 cups boiled red potatoes
4 ears freshly cooked corn

Prepare a medium-hot barbecue fire in a covered grill. Oil the grill rack or coat with a nonstick vegetable spray. In a small bowl, whisk together the clam juice, lemon juice, shallots, tarragon, mustard, Pernod, salt, pepper, and 2 tablespoons of the oil.

Split the lobsters in half lengthwise. Remove and discard the gray intestinal tract, the gills, and the sand sac. Reserve any red roe or green tomalley that you find, and stir it into the vinaigrette. Crack the lobster claws. Brush the cut and exposed lobster meat with the remaining ½ tablespoon of oil.

Grill the lobsters, cut sides down and with the grill covered, 4 minutes. Turn and grill 4 minutes more. Turn again and grill until the lobster meat is translucent throughout, but still juicy, about 3 to 4 minutes more.

Drizzle the cut sides of the lobster with the vinaigrette and serve garnished with the lemon wedges and tarragon sprigs. Serve the potatoes and corn on a separate plate for easier eating.

CALORIES	412.94 KCAL	PROTEIN	31.74 GM
TOTAL FAT	10.99 GM	SATURATED FAT	1.54 GM
SODIUM	726.78 MG	CHOLESTEROL	89.89 MG
CARBOHYDRATE	48.72 GM		

% calories from fat: 23.50%

GRILLED SHRIMP AND PEPPERS ON SPINACH FETTUCCINE

~ ~ ~ ~ ~ ~ ~ ~ ~

4 servings

The sweet smokiness of grilled vegetables and the gorgeous look of grilled shellfish play well against the light sauce on the fettuccine. This is a dish worthy of your finest guests, but it takes almost no time to prepare.

3 teaspoons extra-virgin olive oil
2 cloves garlic, minced
1 (14½-ounce) can Italian-style stewed tomatoes
1 cup dry white wine
1 cup bottled clam juice
¼ teaspoon dried hot red pepper flakes
3 tablespoons chopped fresh basil
12 ounces large or jumbo shrimp, peeled and deveined
1 large yellow or orange bell pepper, quartered
1 large sweet onion, such as Vidalia, cut horizontally into
  ¼-inch slices
8 littleneck or other clams in the shell, scrubbed
1 pound spinach fettuccine, freshly cooked and drained

Prepare a medium-hot barbecue fire. Oil the grill rack or coat with a nonstick vegetable spray.

In a large skillet, heat 1 teaspoon of the oil and sauté the garlic 30 seconds over medium heat. Add the tomatoes with their juices, wine, clam juice, and pepper flakes. Simmer 5 to 8 minutes until reduced by about one third. Stir in the basil. Keep the sauce warm over low heat until ready to continue. (Or make up to 3 hours ahead and rewarm before continuing.)

Thread the shrimp onto skewers, then rub with 1 teaspoon oil. Rub the pepper and onion with the remaining 1 teaspoon oil. Grill the pepper and onion, turning once, about 8 minutes, until tinged with brown and softened. Grill the clams and shrimp, turning the shrimp once, 3 to 5 minutes, until the clams open and the shrimp are opaque and cooked through. (Discard any clams that do not open.)

Pour the sauce over the hot pasta. Add the onion and pepper and toss to mix well. Arrange the shrimp and clams in the shell on top of the pasta.

CALORIES	669.46 KCAL	PROTEIN	37.04 GM
TOTAL FAT	10.18 GM	SATURATED FAT	1.88 GM
SODIUM	699.49 MG	CHOLESTEROL	222.73 MG
CARBOHYDRATE	97.62 GM		

% calories from fat: 14.53%

GRILLED CIOPPINO

8 servings

This is a grill lover's interpretation of the classic San Francisco fish stew (which is an interpretation of the French bouillabaisse). Use almost any combination you like, but clams, shrimp, and firm white-fish make a pretty presentation.

1½ *tablespoons extra-virgin olive oil*
1 *large onion, chopped*
2 *cloves garlic, minced*
1 *(14½-ounce) can stewed tomatoes*
1½ *cups bottled clam juice*
¾ *cup dry white wine*
1 ½ *teaspoons dried marjoram*
1 ½ *teaspoons dried thyme*
¼ *to* ½ *teaspoon dried hot red pepper flakes*
12 *large shrimp, peeled and deveined*
1 *pound halibut or monkfish*
1 *red bell pepper, quartered*
12 *clams in the shell, such as littlenecks, scrubbed*
2 *tablespoons Pernod*

In a 3- or 4-quart saucepan, heat 1 tablespoon of the oil. Stir in the onion and garlic, cover the saucepan, and cook over medium-low heat, stirring occasionally, about 8 minutes, until the onion is softened. Add the tomatoes and juices, clam juice, wine, marjoram, thyme, and pepper flakes. Simmer over medium-low heat, partially covered, 15 minutes. (The recipe can be made to this point early in the day and reheated to finish.)

Prepare a medium-hot barbecue fire. Oil the grill rack or coat with a nonstick vegetable spray.

Rub the shrimp, fish, and bell pepper with the remaining ½ tablespoon (or more) of the oil.

Grill the clams, fish, and pepper, turning once or twice, 8 to 10 minutes, until clams open, fish is just cooked through, and pepper is lightly charred and softened. (Discard any clams that do not open.) Thread the shrimp onto skewers and grill, turning once, 4 to 5 minutes, until just cooked through. Cut the pepper into strips and cut the fish into 6 pieces.

Reheat the soup base and add the Pernod, grilled pepper, shrimp, and fish. Simmer about 1 minute to heat through. Ladle into shallow bowls and garnish with the clams in the shell.

CALORIES	183.27 KCAL	PROTEIN	20.89 GM
TOTAL FAT	4.69 GM	SATURATED FAT	.66 GM
SODIUM	309.94 MG	CHOLESTEROL	63.76 MG
CARBOHYDRATE	8.97 GM		

% calories from fat: 26.11%

BIRDS

Barbecued chicken is synonymous with summer in America. Across the country, nearly every backyard cookout includes a heaping platter of crusty charbroiled chicken drumsticks, thighs, breasts, and wings. If you come from the Midwest, as I do, the chicken would be slathered with a tomato-based barbecue sauce, but in my adopted home of New England, I have learned to glaze my chicken with a molasses sauce. During a stint living in the South, I had a tasty brush with a vinegar-based moppin' sauce, and time spent in the Southwest taught me the value of a peppery dry rub.

But it is only recently that I realized all these favorite regional treatments can be applied to low-fat skinless chicken breasts, either on or off the bone.

Furthermore, now that we know turkey is more than a November word association, I have discovered that this low-fat big bird takes on a whole new and far more contemporary identity when paired with the grill. In addition, turkey's popularity has led to its availability far more than ever before. We now have turkey breast fillets, turkey steaks, ground turkey, and even turkey sausages and frankfurters, all of which take very well to grilling.

In both chicken and turkey, the white breast meat is the leanest part of the bird. Because the skin contains most of the fat, skinless breasts are preferred. When the delicate white meat loses its natural skin protection, it is subject to burning and drying out during cooking. To avoid both, brush lightly with oil or marinate briefly to form a protective coating and cook over a medium or medium-hot fire. Check carefully to prevent overcooking. Breast meat is done when it is white to the center and juices run clear when meat is pricked. This happens faster than you think—usually 10 minutes or less for a boneless and skinless chicken breast half. In the case of ground chicken or turkey and turkey sausage, be sure to check the label for fat content, since some suppliers sneak in extra fat and fattier dark meat. Go for the leanest you can find—about 97 percent fat free if possible.

GRILLED ROSEMARY AND LEMON CHICKEN MARSALA

 ≀ ≀ ≀ ≀ ≀ ≀ ≀ ≀ ≀

4 servings

This sophisticated little dish is perfect for a summer dinner party. An elegant raspberry sorbet (page 158), garnished with a sprinkling of fresh blueberries, is the perfect finishing touch.

¼ *cup dry marsala*
2 tablespoons fresh lemon juice
2 teaspoons extra-virgin olive oil
1 clove garlic, minced
1 tablespoon grated lemon peel
1 tablespoon chopped fresh rosemary or 1 teaspoon dried
½ *teaspoon salt*
¼ *teaspoon freshly ground black pepper*
4 skinless, boneless chicken breast halves (each about 5 ounces)
8 thin lemon slices
8 rosemary sprigs, optional

In a shallow dish just large enough to hold the chicken, combine the marsala, lemon juice, oil, garlic, lemon peel, rosemary, salt, and pepper. Use your hands to flatten the chicken to an even thickness of about ½ inch. Place in the marinade, turning to coat both sides. Let stand 30 minutes at room temperature or up to 2 hours in the refrigerator. Add the lemon slices to the marinade during the last 15 minutes of marinating time. Discard the marinade, reserving the lemon slices.

Prepare a medium-hot barbecue fire. Lightly oil the grill rack or coat with a nonstick vegetable spray. Just before cooking, dampen 4 of the optional rosemary sprigs and toss them onto the coals. Grill the chicken, turning once, about 6 to 8 minutes, until the meat is white throughout. Grill the lemon slices near the edge of the fire about 1 minute per side, until lightly tinged with brown.

Serve the chicken garnished with the lemon slices and the remaining 4 rosemary sprigs, if you are using them.

CALORIES	182.99 KCAL	PROTEIN	32.93 GM
TOTAL FAT	2.94 GM	SATURATED FAT	.61 GM
SODIUM	229.27 MG	CHOLESTEROL	82.21 MG
CARBOHYDRATE	2.96 GM		

% calories from fat: 15.56%

MOLASSES MUSTARD CHICKEN

ʔ ʔ ʔ ʔ ʔ ʔ ʔ ʔ ʔ

4 servings

Set a platter of these chicken breasts on a buffet table along with some potato salad and coleslaw (see Accompaniments and Desserts, pages 151 and 155) for an old-fashioned family summer supper.

2 tablespoons molasses
2 tablespoons Dijon mustard
1 tablespoon cider vinegar
1 tablespoon chopped fresh thyme or 1 teaspoon dried
4 skinless, boneless chicken breast halves (each about 5 ounces)
2 teaspoons vegetable oil, preferably canola oil
Salt and freshly ground black pepper

In a shallow dish just large enough to hold the chicken, combine the molasses, mustard, vinegar, and thyme. Use your hands to flatten the

continued

chicken to an even thickness of about ½ inch. Rub with the oil on all sides, then sprinkle lightly with salt and generously with pepper. Add to the marinade, turning to coat both sides. Let stand 30 minutes at room temperature or refrigerate up to 2 hours, turning occasionally.

Prepare a medium-hot barbecue fire. Oil the grill rack or coat with a nonstick vegetable spray. Grill the chicken, turning once, for a total of 6 to 8 minutes, until the meat is white throughout.

CALORIES	213.79 KCAL	PROTEIN	32.76 GM
TOTAL FAT	4.54 GM	SATURATED FAT	.62 GM
SODIUM	321.05 MG	CHOLESTEROL	82.21 MG
CARBOHYDRATE	8.48 GM		

% calories from fat: 19.85%

GRILLED SUN-DRIED TOMATO AND BASIL STUFFED CHICKEN

4 servings

Tomatoes and basil are a marriage made in garden heaven. Sun-dried tomatoes have a more intense and naturally smoky sweet flavor than fresh. They come both packed in oil and dried, but the dried are preferable for low-fat cooking, and they taste just as good when rehydrated.

2 ounces sun-dried tomatoes (about 8 small pieces)
½ cup reduced-sodium chicken broth
4 skinless, boneless chicken breast halves (each about 5 ounces)
8 large basil leaves

₹₹₹

Salt and freshly ground black pepper
2 tablespoons balsamic vinegar
1 tablespoon extra-virgin olive oil
1 clove garlic, minced
⅛ teaspoon crushed dried hot red pepper flakes

In a small saucepan on the stovetop, or in a microwave oven, bring the tomatoes and broth just to a boil. Let stand about 15 minutes, until the tomatoes are softened. Remove the tomatoes and reserve any remaining broth. Cut the tomatoes in half.

Use a small sharp knife to cut as large a pocket as possible in each chicken breast, taking care not to cut all the way through. Divide the rehydrated tomatoes and the basil among the chicken, stuffing them into the pockets. Sprinkle the chicken lightly with salt and pepper.

In a shallow dish just large enough to hold the chicken, combine the reserved broth, vinegar, oil, garlic, and red pepper. Let stand 30 minutes at room temperature or up to 2 hours in the refrigerator. Drain and discard the marinade.

Prepare a medium-hot fire. Lightly oil the grill or coat with a non-stick vegetable spray. Grill the chicken, turning once with a spatula, 8 to 10 minutes, until the meat is white throughout.

Serve warm or at room temperature, cut into crosswise sections and fanned out if desired.

CALORIES	238.44 KCAL	PROTEIN	35.28 GM
TOTAL FAT	5.77 GM	SATURATED FAT	.98 GM
SODIUM	191.79 MG	CHOLESTEROL	82.21 MG
CARBOHYDRATE	11.55 GM		

% calories from fat: 21.70%

GRILLED MINTED YOGURT CHICKEN

ι ι ι ι ι ι ι ι ι

4 servings

Nonfat plain yogurt is a terrific marinade. The milk solids and sugars add flavor to the chicken as it caramelizes to a rich golden color over the grill. For more intense flavor, toss a handful of dampened mint onto the grill just before cooking the chicken. Roasted or grilled new potatoes and lightly stewed fresh tomatoes complement the dish nicely.

1 cup nonfat plain yogurt
½ cup chopped mint
1 large clove garlic, minced
½ teaspoon ground cumin
½ teaspoon salt
⅛ teaspoon cayenne
4 skinless, boneless chicken breast halves (each about 5 ounces)
Handful of mint sprigs, optional

In a shallow dish just large enough to hold the chicken, combine the yogurt, mint, garlic, cumin, salt, and cayenne. Use your hands to flatten the chicken to an even thickness of about ½ inch. Add to the yogurt marinade, turning to coat both sides. Let stand 30 minutes at room temperature or up to 2 hours in the refrigerator.

Prepare a medium-hot barbecue fire. Lightly oil the grill rack or coat with a nonstick vegetable spray. Just before cooking, dampen all but 4 of the optional mint sprigs and toss them onto the coals.

Grill the chicken, turning once, for a total of 6 to 8 minutes, until the meat is white throughout. Garnish the dish with the reserved mint sprigs, if you are using them.

CALORIES	191.61 KCAL	PROTEIN	36.15 GM
TOTAL FAT	1.93 GM	SATURATED FAT	.54 GM
SODIUM	409.24 MG	CHOLESTEROL	83.34 MG
CARBOHYDRATE	5.05 GM		

% calories from fat: 9.53%

MAPLE CIDER CHICKEN AND PUMPKIN KABOBS

ι ι ι ι ι ι ι ι ι

4 servings

Small "sugar" pumpkins have a short season, but are just wonderful cooked on the grill. If not available, use Hubbard or acorn squash. Seeds from both sugar pumpkins and the larger "jack-o'-lanterns" make excellent snacks when roasted on a baking sheet in a 350° F. oven until crisp, lightly browned, and fragrant. Sprinkle them with salt.

1 small sugar pumpkin (about 1 pound)
¼ cup cider vinegar
¼ cup maple syrup
2 teaspoons Dijon mustard
2 teaspoons vegetable oil, preferably canola oil
2 teaspoons dried leaf sage or 2 tablespoons chopped fresh

continued

4 skinless, boneless chicken breast halves (each about 5 ounces)
Salt and freshly ground black pepper

Cut the pumpkin in half and remove the seeds. Use a small sharp knife to peel the pumpkin, then cut the flesh into 1½-inch cubes. Place in a microwave-safe baking dish and add about 3 tablespoons water. Cover tightly and microwave on high 4 to 5 minutes, until just fork tender. Alternatively, simmer in water on the stovetop about 8 minutes, until just fork tender. Set aside.

In a small saucepan, simmer the vinegar, maple syrup, and mustard about 5 minutes, until lightly reduced. Stir in the oil and sage, then pour into a shallow dish just large enough to hold the chicken. Let cool.

Cut the chicken into 1- to 1½-inch chunks. Sprinkle lightly with salt and pepper, then place the chicken in the marinade, stirring to coat completely. Let stand 30 minutes at room temperature or up to 2 hours in the refrigerator, stirring occasionally. Add the pumpkin cubes to the marinade during the last 20 minutes.

Prepare a medium-hot barbecue fire. Lightly oil the grill rack or coat with a nonstick cooking spray.

Thread the chicken and pumpkin onto metal skewers. Grill, turning once, for a total of 6 to 8 minutes, until the chicken meat is white throughout.

CALORIES	254.41 KCAL	PROTEIN	33.55 GM
TOTAL FAT	4.32 GM	SATURATED FAT	.67 GM
SODIUM	169.98 MG	CHOLESTEROL	82.21 MG
CARBOHYDRATE	19.80 GM		

% calories from fat: 15.41%

WEST INDIES CHICKEN WITH GRILLED PINEAPPLE SALSA

ι ι ι ι ι ι ι ι ι

6 servings

Salsa is the favored condiment of today's healthier diet, and the usual tomato and onion version is just the beginning. This pineapple salsa is as delicious with grilled pork tenderloin or swordfish steaks as it is with quick-cooking chicken or turkey cutlets. For ease in preparation, buy sliced fresh pineapple in the produce section or at the salad bar in your market.

1 red onion, chopped
1 jalapeño, minced
¼ cup chopped cilantro
½ cup unsweetened pineapple juice
1 tablespoon fresh lime juice
1 tablespoon red wine vinegar
2 teaspoons paprika
2 teaspoons dried oregano
2 teaspoons dried thyme
½ teaspoon salt
½ teaspoon cayenne
1½ pounds thinly sliced chicken or turkey breast cutlets
¾ pound fresh pineapple slices (about 1 small pineapple)
2 teaspoons vegetable oil, preferably canola oil

In a medium mixing bowl, combine the onion, jalapeño, cilantro, pineapple and lime juices, and vinegar. Set the salsa aside at room temperature. In a small bowl, combine the paprika, oregano, thyme,

continued

salt, and cayenne. Use your fingers to coat the chicken and the pineapple slices lightly with the oil, then sprinkle the chicken with the seasoning blend.

Prepare a hot barbecue fire. Oil the grill rack or coat with a nonstick vegetable spray. Grill the chicken, turning once, until just cooked through, about 4 to 6 minutes total. Grill the pineapple until it is lightly charred, about 2 to 3 minutes total.

Coarsely dice the pineapple slices and add to the salsa. Arrange the chicken on a platter or individual plates in overlapping slices. Spoon some of the salsa on top and serve the remainder on the side.

CALORIES	196.76 KCAL	PROTEIN	27.21 GM
TOTAL FAT	3.38 GM	SATURATED FAT	.51 GM
SODIUM	261.22 MG	CHOLESTEROL	65.83 MG
CARBOHYDRATE	14.13 GM		

% calories from fat: 15.53%

THAI GRILLED CHICKEN SALAD

4 servings

When I first whiffed Thai fish sauce, I couldn't believe people actually ate it. I've since learned that this, one of the most common condiments on the Thai table, is a delicious ingredient in marinades and salad dressings. Over the last several years, Thai food has taken the country by storm, and for good reason—it tastes terrific and is often quite low-fat. As a result of the popularity, such Thai ingredients as fish sauce and lemongrass are increasingly available. If you can't find lemongrass, substitute 1 teaspoon grated lemon peel or 1 tablespoon chopped fresh cilantro, an herb with a lemony taste.

ʔʔʔ

1 stalk lemongrass
¼ cup reduced-sodium chicken broth
3 tablespoons fresh lime juice
2 tablespoons extra-virgin olive oil
2 tablespoons Thai fish sauce (nam pla)
1 tablespoon reduced-sodium soy sauce
1 tablespoon honey
2 large cloves garlic, minced
3 tablespoons chopped mint
2 tablespoons chopped basil
2 teaspoons minced jalapeño
4 skinless, boneless chicken breast halves (each about 5 ounces)
8 cups thinly sliced iceberg lettuce
1 large yellow bell pepper, seeded and thinly sliced
1 seedless cucumber, halved lengthwise and thinly sliced
8 cherry tomatoes, halved

Peel and discard the outer three layers of the lemongrass stalk. Finely chop the white interior of the lemongrass stalk to make about 1 tablespoon.

In a small bowl, combine the chopped lemongrass, broth, lime juice, oil, fish sauce, soy sauce, honey, garlic, mint, basil, and jalapeños. Pour about half of the mixture into a shallow dish just large enough to hold the chicken. Reserve the remainder to use as the dressing for the salad.

Use your hands to flatten the chicken to an even thickness of about ½ inch. Place in the marinade, turning to coat completely. Let stand 30 minutes at room temperature or up to 2 hours in the refrigerator, turning occasionally.

Prepare a medium-hot barbecue fire. Oil the grill rack or coat with a nonstick vegetable spray. Grill the chicken, turning once, for a total of 6 to 8 minutes, until the meat is white throughout.

Toss the lettuce with the reserved marinade, then arrange on indi-

continued

vidual plates. Slice the chicken crosswise and arrange in overlapping slices on the lettuce. Garnish with the bell pepper, cucumber, and tomatoes.

CALORIES	301.55 KCAL	PROTEIN	36.78 GM
TOTAL FAT	9.97 GM	SATURATED FAT	1.62 GM
SODIUM	298.39 MG	CHOLESTEROL	82.21 MG
CARBOHYDRATE	16.51 GM		

% calories from fat: 29.62%

Down-Home Finger-Lickin' Barbecued Chicken

8 servings

This recipe makes enough brush-on to serve some alongside the chicken. For maximum safety, keep the serving sauce separate from the sauce that you are brushing on the chicken. Add wet hickory chips to the fire if you like a hickory-flavored barbecue. Chicken on the bone is more flavorful and prompts finger-lickin' more than boneless breasts.

½ *cup reduced-sodium chicken or vegetable broth*
½ *cup finely chopped onion*
⅓ *cup finely chopped celery*
2 *teaspoons dry mustard*
¼ *teaspoon celery seeds*
1 *cup bottled chili sauce*
1 *cup beer*

1 bay leaf, broken in half
2 tablespoons molasses
1 tablespoon Worcestershire sauce
Salt and freshly ground black pepper
¼ to ½ teaspoon Tabasco or other hot sauce
8 chicken breast halves on the bone (each about 7 ounces)
2 teaspoons vegetable oil, preferably canola oil

Place the broth, onion, and celery in a medium nonreactive saucepan. Cover and simmer 5 minutes, until the vegetables are softened. Stir in the mustard and celery seeds, then stir in the chili sauce, beer, bay leaf, molasses, and Worcestershire sauce. Simmer gently, uncovered, stirring often, 20 to 30 minutes, until the sauce is lightly thickened. Taste and season with salt, pepper, and the Tabasco sauce. Discard the bay leaf. Use the sauce immediately or cover and refrigerate for up to a week.

Prepare a medium-hot barbecue fire. Lightly oil the grill rack or coat with a nonstick vegetable spray.

Use your hands to pull off and discard the chicken skin, then cut off and discard all of the visible fat. Rub all sides of the chicken with the oil, then sprinkle lightly with salt and pepper.

Transfer one half of the sauce to a small bowl and set near the grill for brushing. Grill the chicken 3 minutes per side, then brush with some of the sauce and continue to grill, turning two or three times and brushing with more sauce, for an additional 10 to 12 minutes, until the meat is white throughout.

Discard the brushing sauce, and serve the chicken hot with the reserved serving sauce.

CALORIES	216.53 KCAL	PROTEIN	31.21 GM
TOTAL FAT	3.07 GM	SATURATED FAT	.50 GM
SODIUM	610.86 MG	CHOLESTEROL	74.81 MG
CARBOHYDRATE	14.73 GM		

% calories from fat: 13.07%

Grilled Greek Chicken Salad

ʔ ʔ ʔ ʔ ʔ ʔ ʔ ʔ ʔ

4 servings

I really love the foods of the Mediterranean, especially since they so naturally lend themselves to light, low-fat preparation. If you use skewers that are about 8 inches long, the chicken and vegetables in this Greek recipe will make a pretty presentation set directly on the orzo salad. Vanilla frozen yogurt drizzled with an anise-flavored liqueur is my dessert choice.

2 teaspoons grated lemon zest
5 tablespoons fresh lemon juice
2 teaspoons dried oregano
½ teaspoon salt
¾ teaspoon freshly ground black pepper
1 pound skinless, boneless chicken breasts
1 medium zucchini (about 6 ounces)
1 large red bell pepper
1¼ cups orzo
½ cup reduced-sodium chicken broth
1 tablespoon white wine vinegar
½ cup chopped parsley
½ cup chopped scallions
¼ cup chopped mint
½ cup drained canned chickpeas
8 large leaves romaine lettuce

In a shallow dish just large enough to hold the chicken and vegetables, combine 1 teaspoon of the lemon zest, 4 tablespoons of the lemon juice, 1 teaspoon of the oregano, and ¼ teaspoon each of the salt and pepper. Cut the chicken into 1- to 1½-inch chunks, the zucchini into ½-inch slices, and the bell pepper into 8 strips. Place the chicken, zucchini, and pepper in the marinade, turning to coat completely. Let stand at room temperature 30 minutes or refrigerate up to 2 hours.

Meanwhile cook the orzo in a large pot of boiling, salted water 9 to 11 minutes, until al dente. Drain well and turn into a large bowl.

In a small mixing bowl, whisk together the broth, vinegar, and the remaining lemon juice, lemon zest, oregano, pepper, and salt. Pour over the warm orzo and stir to mix well. Stir in the parsley, scallions, mint, and chickpeas. Let cool to room temperature.

Prepare a medium-hot barbecue fire. Oil the grill rack or coat with a nonstick vegetable spray. Alternately thread the chicken, zucchini, and pepper onto 4 metal skewers.

Grill, turning once or twice, 6 to 8 minutes, until the chicken is white throughout and the vegetables are lightly charred and softened.

On a large platter or individual plates, make a bed of the romaine leaves. Spoon the orzo salad over, then arrange the skewers on top of the salad.

CALORIES	412.64 KCAL	PROTEIN	37.07 GM
TOTAL FAT	3.34 GM	SATURATED FAT	.55 GM
SODIUM	482.94 MG	CHOLESTEROL	65.83 MG
CARBOHYDRATE	57.04 GM		

% calories from fat: 7.39%

TANDOOR-STYLE CHICKEN

ι ι ι ι ι ι ι ι ι

4 servings

A backyard barbecue is never going to be a tandoor oven, but this marinade sure does a good job of mimicking the exotic flavors of the Indian specialty. Steamed broccoli and carrots sprinkled with chopped coriander, and basmati rice, are traditional accompaniments.

continued

1 *cup nonfat plain yogurt*
1 *tablespoon fresh lemon juice*
1 *tablespoon grated fresh ginger*
2 *cloves garlic, minced*
2 *teaspoons ground cardamom*
2 *teaspoons ground cumin*
¾ *teaspoon turmeric*
½ *teaspoon salt*
¼ *teaspoon cayenne*
4 *skinless, boneless chicken breast halves (each about 5 ounces)*

In a shallow dish just large enough to hold the chicken, combine the yogurt, lemon juice, ginger, garlic, cardamom, cumin, turmeric, salt, and cayenne. Use your hands to flatten the chicken to an even thickness of about ½ inch. Place in the marinade, turning to coat both sides. Let stand 30 minutes at room temperature or up to 2 hours in the refrigerator, turning occasionally.

Prepare a medium-hot barbecue fire. Lightly oil the grill or coat with a nonstick vegetable spray. Grill the chicken, turning once, for a total of 6 to 8 minutes, until the chicken is white throughout.

CALORIES	178.09 KCAL	PROTEIN	34.54 GM
TOTAL FAT	1.96 GM	SATURATED FAT	.50 GM
SODIUM	250.35 MG	CHOLESTEROL	82.77 MG
CARBOHYDRATE	3.35 GM		

% calories from fat: 10.42%

GRILL-SMOKED TURKEY WITH CURRIED PEACH SALSA

~ ~ ~ ~ ~ ~ ~ ~ ~

6 servings

If you have a smoker, by all means use it here, following the manufacturer's directions for smoking. In fact, smoke a whole turkey breast and save the leftovers for great sandwiches and salads. The salsa is also good with grilled fish or chicken breasts.

6 to 8 handfuls hickory chips
½ turkey breast on the bone (about 2 pounds)
Salt and freshly ground black pepper

CURRIED PEACH SALSA

2 large peaches
½ cup chopped red onion
2 tablespoons chopped fresh cilantro
2 tablespoons fresh lime juice
1 tablespoon honey
½ teaspoon grated lime peel
½ teaspoon curry powder
½ teaspoon freshly ground black pepper

Soak the hickory chips in water at least 30 minutes.

Prepare an indirect barbecue fire. If using a charcoal grill, prepare the fire, then use tongs to move the coals to the perimeter of the grill. Set a disposable foil pan in the center of the firebox and push the coals around the pan. If using a gas grill, preheat according to manu-

continued

facturer's directions for an indirect fire, using wood chips. Lightly oil the grill rack or coat with a nonstick vegetable spray.

Sprinkle all sides of the turkey generously with salt and pepper. Just before cooking, toss half of the wet wood chips onto the coals. Place the turkey, skin side down, on the grill rack over the drip pan. Grill 20 minutes, then turn with tongs and grill an additional 30 to 35 minutes, until an internal temperature registers 170° F. on an instant-read thermometer.

While the turkey is grilling, prepare the salsa. Peel the peaches and cut into ½-inch chunks. In a medium bowl, combine the peaches with the onion, cilantro, lime juice, honey, lime peel, curry powder, and pepper. Let stand 30 minutes at room temperature or refrigerate up to 2 hours before serving.

When the turkey is done, let it cool 15 minutes, then remove and discard all of the skin. Slice the turkey and serve warm or at room temperature with the salsa.

CALORIES	174.56 KCAL	PROTEIN	30.05 GM
TOTAL FAT	.85 GM	SATURATED FAT	.25 GM
SODIUM	61.20 MG	CHOLESTEROL	74.12 MG
CARBOHYDRATE	10.76 GM		

% calories from fat: 4.47%

GRILLED TURKEY STEAKS WITH CRANBERRY-CURRANT SALSA

ι ι ι ι ι ι ι ι ι

6 servings

Turkey "steaks" are crosswise cuts of boned turkey breasts that are about ½ inch thick. You can substitute turkey breast fillets if you wish. The salsa is also delicious with Grill-Smoked Turkey (page 87) or as a condiment with grilled pork chops. Complete the New England theme to this dinner with Yankee Maple Baked Beans (page 156) and end with Huckleberry Cobbler (page 161).

CRANBERRY-CURRANT SALSA

1½ cups (6 ounces) fresh cranberries
½ cup sugar
¼ cup dried currants
2 tablespoons freshly grated or prepared horseradish

1¼ pounds turkey breast steaks
2 teaspoons canola oil
Salt and freshly ground black pepper
2 teaspoons dried, crumbled leaf sage

To make the salsa, coarsely chop the cranberries in a food processor. Add the sugar, currants, and horseradish and process briefly to blend. Refrigerate the salsa at least 1 hour and up to 48 hours before using.

Prepare a medium-hot barbecue fire. Lightly oil the grill rack or coat with a nonstick vegetable spray.

Rub the turkey all over with the oil, then season with salt, pepper, and the sage. Grill the turkey, turning once, for a total of 6 to 8 minutes, until the meat is white throughout.

Serve the turkey with the salsa spooned over it.

CALORIES	216.44 KCAL	PROTEIN	23.70 GM
TOTAL FAT	2.20 GM	SATURATED FAT	.30 GM
SODIUM	47.46 MG	CHOLESTEROL	58.64 MG
CARBOHYDRATE	25.26 GM		

% calories from fat: 9.18%

GRILLED TURKEY ITALIAN SAUSAGE SUBS WITH GRILLED VINEGAR PEPPERS

ﾞ ﾞ ﾞ ﾞ ﾞ ﾞ ﾞ ﾞ ﾞ

8 servings

Turkey Italian sausage is fabulous, but brands vary in seasoning. Taste several to find the one you like best. This sandwich will be a hit with the whole family, especially if you serve it with a side dish of spaghetti and tomato sauce, a tossed salad, and garlic bread sticks.

1 green bell pepper
1 red bell pepper
1 large sweet onion, such as Vidalia
1 tablespoon extra-virgin olive oil
1 pound turkey Italian sausage links
1 to 2 tablespoons balsamic vinegar
Salt and freshly ground black pepper
8 Italian rolls, each about 4 inches long, split

Prepare a medium-hot barbecue fire. Lightly oil the grill rack or coat with a nonstick vegetable spray.

Cut the peppers into quarters, and the onion into crosswise slices about ¼ inch thick. Brush all sides of the peppers and the onion slices with the oil.

Grill the peppers, onions, and sausages 7 to 9 minutes, turning often, until the peppers and onions are softened and lightly charred, and the sausages are browned on all sides.

Cut the sausage into ¼-inch slices and place in a bowl. Thinly slice the peppers and separate the onions into rings and add to the sausage. Sprinkle with the vinegar and salt and pepper to taste, then toss to combine.

To serve, spoon the sausage, peppers, and onions and any accumulated juices into the Italian rolls.

CALORIES	260.42 KCAL	PROTEIN	13.10 GM
TOTAL FAT	8.53 GM	SATURATED FAT	.70 GM
SODIUM	580.92 MG	CHOLESTEROL	40.71 MG
CARBOHYDRATE	32.77 GM		

% calories from fat: 29.49%

GRILLED TURKEY CLUB SANDWICH

4 servings

This is a contemporary version of an old favorite. Make some Grilled Potato "Chips" (page 32) to replace the usual potato chips if you wish. If you want the real traditional look, stick a small radish on a toothpick to secure the sandwich quarters.

⅓ cup low-fat or nonfat mayonnaise
1 tablespoon Dijon mustard
1 pound thinly sliced turkey breast cutlets
2 teaspoons extra-virgin olive oil
Salt and freshly ground black pepper
1 teaspoon dried leaf thyme
*12 slices thin-sliced whole wheat sandwich bread, toasted or
    lightly grilled*
1 ounce well-trimmed prosciutto, very thinly sliced
1 bunch arugula, trimmed
2 medium tomatoes, seeded and thinly sliced
1 red onion, very thinly sliced

continued

In a small dish, combine the mayonnaise and mustard. Refrigerate until ready to use.

Prepare a hot barbecue fire. Lightly oil the grill rack or coat with a nonstick vegetable spray.

Rub the turkey all over with the oil, then season with salt and pepper, and the thyme.

Grill the turkey, turning once, for a total of 4 to 6 minutes, until golden brown.

Assemble 4 triple-decker sandwiches by spreading the toast with the flavored mayonnaise, then making sandwiches with the turkey, prosciutto, arugula, tomatoes, and onion. Cut each sandwich into quarters to serve.

CALORIES	465.15 KCAL	PROTEIN	40.55 GM
TOTAL FAT	13.45 GM	SATURATED FAT	2.92 GM
SODIUM	881.76 MG	CHOLESTEROL	82.66 MG
CARBOHYDRATE	48.55 GM		

% calories from fat: 25.35%

Tarragon Turkey Burgers

6 servings

Ground turkey burgers have come into vogue primarily because turkey is a low-fat alternative to beef, but I think they are a welcome and sophisticated change, as demonstrated in this light and elegant burger. If you like, spoon some mushrooms braised in chicken stock over the cooked turkey patties.

1 egg white, lightly beaten
1¼ pounds ground turkey
½ cup fine fresh white bread crumbs
¼ cup chopped chervil or parsley
¼ cup finely chopped shallots
1½ tablespoons chopped fresh tarragon or 1 teaspoon dried
½ teaspoon salt
¼ teaspoon freshly ground black pepper
12 slices French bread, diagonally cut about ½ inch thick
2 tablespoons Dijon mustard
6 slices tomato
6 leaves Boston or other soft lettuce
4 sprigs tarragon, optional

Prepare a medium-hot barbecue fire. Lightly oil the grill rack or coat with a nonstick vegetable spray.

In a mixing bowl, use your hands to combine the egg white, turkey, bread crumbs, chervil, shallots, tarragon, salt, and pepper. Form into 6 patties, each about 4 inches in diameter. Brush one side of the bread slices with about half of the mustard.

Grill the turkey patties, turning once, until white throughout but still juicy, about 12 to 14 minutes. A few minutes before the turkey is done, set the bread at the edges of the grill and cook, turning once, until lightly toasted, about 2 minutes total.

Brush the tops of the turkey patties with the remaining mustard. Make sandwiches with the grilled toasts, burgers, tomato, and lettuce. Garnish the sandwiches with the tarragon sprigs, if desired.

CALORIES	311.00 KCAL	PROTEIN	22.46 GM
TOTAL FAT	10.24 GM	SATURATED FAT	2.57 GM
SODIUM	703.11 MG	CHOLESTEROL	58.57 MG
CARBOHYDRATE	30.61 GM		

% calories from fat: 30.27%

MEAT

For some people, meat is nothing more than a four-letter word. Not me. I like it. However, I do confess that a big rare steak or a cold-in-the-middle burger never held much appeal. I like my meat to have character—a barbecued brisket or a grilled pork chop or a kabob of savory charred lamb. With leanings like this, it is only natural that my favorite meat cooking methods have always involved the grill.

A lot of people still enjoy grilled meats—hamburgers and hot dogs are probably the most commonly grilled foods in the whole country. Now that Americans are cutting back on overall dietary fat, many fear that these favorites will have to go. They do not; they just have to change. In my mind, the principle of "less is more" applies to meat cookery. A big hunk of plain meat has "less" flavor and satisfaction, while there is a lot "more" to a little steak with a lot of grilled onions on a freshly toasted bun. The recipes that follow offer modest servings of highly seasoned lean meats.

I recommend buying quality fresh meat from a reputable butcher who knows how to properly trim off all the extra fat. Although there is nothing wrong with buying and freezing meat, I find that juices are lost in the thawing process, which is problematic for grilling, a dry-heat cooking method. Lean meat, as well as previously frozen meat, tends to dry out if overcooked, so watch carefully while grilling over medium-hot coals in order to sear the exterior and seal in the juices while the meat cooks throughout.

New Braunfels Barbecued Brisket

〜 〜 〜 〜 〜 〜 〜 〜 〜

8 to 10 servings

This version of the famous Texas barbecue starts with a very well trimmed brisket. The oven roasting helps tenderize and retain the juices of the leaner cut; then the seasoned meat is finished on the grill to give it the classic smokiness and crusty edges. In Texas the sauce is served on the side, but if the sliced meat is simmered in the spicy sauce, then served as a sandwich, it becomes even more tender and tasty, and goes further, too. Serve with grilled corn on the cob and potato salad.

SEASONING MIX AND MEAT

1 teaspoon salt
½ teaspoon freshly ground black pepper
½ teaspoon paprika
½ teaspoon ground allspice
¼ teaspoon cayenne
2½ to 3 pounds beef brisket, trimmed of all visible fat

TEXAS SAUCE

1½ cups bottled chili sauce
¼ cup bottled ketchup
3 tablespoons light brown sugar
3 tablespoons bourbon
2 tablespoons reduced-sodium soy sauce
2 tablespoons cider vinegar
1 large clove garlic, minced
Up to 1 cup juices from meat
¼ to ½ teaspoon Tabasco or other hot sauce

Mesquite chips

8 to 10 kaiser or other sandwich rolls, split

In a small dish, combine the salt, pepper, paprika, allspice, and cayenne. Sprinkle the mixture evenly and generously over all sides of the meat. Refrigerate at least 1 hour or up to 24 hours.

When ready to cook, preheat the oven to 350° F. Wrap the meat in heavy-duty aluminum foil and place in a baking dish. Bake 2 hours, until the meat is tender.

While the meat is baking, make the Texas sauce by bringing the chili sauce, ketchup, brown sugar, bourbon, soy sauce, vinegar, and garlic to a boil in a medium nonreactive saucepan. Lower the heat and simmer 10 minutes. Remove the meat from the oven; unwrap it over the baking dish to retain the cooking juices. Degrease the juices and add up to 1 cup to the sauce. Simmer the sauce an additional 10 minutes.

While the meat is baking, prepare a medium-hot barbecue fire. Oil the grill or coat with a nonstick vegetable spray. Soak the mesquite chips in cold water 30 minutes, then toss them onto the coals just before cooking the meat.

Grill the partially cooked meat about 30 minutes, turning once, until the outside is well browned and crusty and the meat is fork tender. Let the meat rest 10 minutes (or cool and refrigerate up to 24 hours). Thinly slice the meat across the grain and place in overlapping slices in a baking dish, discarding any congealed fat.

Spoon the sauce over the meat, cover the dish with foil, and bake in a 350° F. oven about 30 minutes, until the meat is very hot.

Serve the meat and sauce spooned into the kaiser rolls.

CALORIES	330.20 KCAL	PROTEIN	23.14 GM
TOTAL FAT	10.43 GM	SATURATED FAT	3.43 GM
SODIUM	1,358.94 MG	CHOLESTEROL	60.32 MG
CARBOHYDRATE	32.59 GM		

% calories from fat: 29.63%

STEAK AND GRILLED SUMMER VEGETABLE SALAD

z z z z z z z z z

6 to 8 servings

Today's nutritional guidelines encourage us to eat more vegetables and less meat. Here is a delicious way to do just that. Vary the vegetables according to what looks best at the market. If you have a hinged grill basket, put the vegetables in it to make turning a one-stroke job.

⅓ cup reduced-sodium vegetable broth
¼ cup balsamic vinegar
2 tablespoons extra-virgin olive oil
1 large clove garlic, minced
1 tablespoon chopped fresh oregano or 1 teaspoon dried
¼ teaspoon salt
¼ teaspoon freshly ground black pepper
1 pound top round steak, cut about ¾ inch thick
1 medium zucchini (about 6 ounces)
1 medium crookneck squash (about 6 ounces)
1 red onion
1 small orange or yellow bell pepper
1 small red bell pepper
12 to 16 diagonal slices French bread
2 bunches arugula, washed and dried

In a small dish, whisk together the broth, vinegar, oil, garlic, oregano, salt, and pepper. Set aside half of the vinaigrette for the salad dressing and pour the remainder in a shallow dish just large enough to hold the meat. Place the meat in the marinade, turning to coat completely. Refrigerate at least 2 hours or up to 8 hours, turning occasionally.

Prepare a medium barbecue fire. Oil the grill rack or coat with a nonstick vegetable spray. Cut the zucchini and crookneck squash into long diagonal slices, each about ¼ inch thick. Cut the onion into crosswise slices, each slightly less than ¼ inch thick. Cut each of the peppers into 6 slices.

Remove the meat from the marinade, then brush all of the cut vegetables with some of the marinade. Grill the meat and vegetables, turning once or twice and brushing with more of the marinade, until the vegetables are tender and lightly charred at the edges and the meat is medium rare. The vegetables will take a total of about 8 minutes, but the meat will take only about 6 minutes. Grill the French bread about 30 seconds per side until lightly toasted.

When the meat is cooked, slice it thinly across the grain. Toss the arugula with the reserved vinaigrette, then divide among 6 to 8 serving plates. Arrange the meat and vegetables decoratively atop the greens, and garnish with the grilled French bread.

CALORIES	290.30 KCAL	PROTEIN	22.07 GM
TOTAL FAT	7.96 GM	SATURATED FAT	1.66 GM
SODIUM	483.57 MG	CHOLESTEROL	40.86 MG
CARBOHYDRATE	32.35 GM		

% calories from fat: 24.76%

GRILLED STEAK AND CHARRED ONION SANDWICH

〜 〜 〜 〜 〜 〜 〜 〜 〜

4 servings

When thinly sliced and quickly grilled, lean round steak stays tender and juicy, while onions take on a rich caramelized color and flavor. Together they are one of my favorite grilled sandwiches.

¼ cup dry white wine
2 tablespoons grainy Dijon mustard
1 tablespoon chopped fresh thyme or 1 teaspoon dried
12 ounces very thinly sliced round steak (often called sandwich steak)
Salt and freshly ground black pepper
1 large sweet onion, cut horizontally into 1/4-inch slices
1 teaspoon vegetable oil, preferably canola oil
4 crusty sandwich rolls, such as Portuguese or kaiser rolls
1 small bunch watercress

Prepare a hot barbecue fire. Oil the grill rack or coat with a nonstick vegetable spray.

In a small dish, combine the wine, mustard, and thyme. Set aside. Sprinkle the meat lightly with salt and very generously with pepper. Rub the onion slices with the oil. Split the sandwich rolls.

Grill the meat and the onion, turning both once or twice, until the meat is cooked through and the onion is softened. The meat will take only about 3 minutes, but the onion will take up to 8 minutes to soften. During the last few minutes of grilling, set the rolls, cut side down, at the edge of the grill to lightly toast.

Generously spread the cut sides of the rolls with the mustard mixture, then separate the onion into rings and make sandwiches with the onion rings, meat, and watercress.

CALORIES	356.56 KCAL	PROTEIN	26.34 GM
TOTAL FAT	8.88 GM	SATURATED FAT	2.05 GM
SODIUM	597.39 MG	CHOLESTEROL	49.75 MG
CARBOHYDRATE	39.57 GM		

% calories from fat: 23.26%

CALIFORNIA BURGERS

ι ι ι ι ι ι ι ι ι

8 servings

California, which years ago placed its cooking emphasis on fresh fruits, vegetables, and grains, was ahead of its time, both in taste and in what is now accepted as good nutrition. These burgers, in which the meat has been "stretched" by a little cooked rice or couscous (use whatever you might have on hand), are also livened with lots of colorful, fresh, healthy goodies.

1 cup cooked brown or white rice or couscous
1 tablespoon reduced-sodium soy sauce
1 teaspoon hot pepper sauce
1¼ pounds lean ground chuck
½ cup nonfat plain yogurt
2 tablespoons prepared honey mustard
8 whole wheat pita breads
1 cup chopped fresh tomato
1 cup alfalfa sprouts

continued

Prepare a medium-hot barbecue fire. Oil the grill rack or coat with a nonstick vegetable spray.

In a mixing bowl, combine the rice, soy sauce, and hot pepper sauce. Add the beef and mix gently but thoroughly. Divide the meat mixture into 8 portions and gently form each into a pattie, about 4 inches in diameter. In a small dish, stir together the yogurt and mustard. Reserve.

Grill the meat, turning once, to desired degree of doneness, about 5 to 8 minutes per side for medium rare. About a minute before the burgers are done, set the pita breads at the edge of the grill to warm slightly.

Use a sharp knife to cut pockets in the pitas about halfway around the circumference of the breads. Spread the pocket with the flavored yogurt. Insert the burgers, and garnish with the tomato and sprouts.

CALORIES	370.02 KCAL	PROTEIN	21.45 GM
TOTAL FAT	12.30 GM	SATURATED FAT	4.41 GM
SODIUM	541.44 MG	CHOLESTEROL	46.77 MG
CARBOHYDRATE	44.75 GM		

% calories from fat: 29.48%

SCANDINAVIAN GRILLED VEAL BURGERS

≀ ≀ ≀ ≀ ≀ ≀ ≀ ≀ ≀

6 servings

Fresh bread crumbs and an egg white keep the veal moist while adding texture to the burgers. Fresh dill is easy to come by, and far better than its dried counterpart. Serve the burgers in soft sandwich rolls or on a bed of fresh poppy seed noodles.

12 ounces lean ground veal
¾ cup fine fresh white or whole wheat bread crumbs
2 tablespoons chopped dill
2 tablespoons chopped parsley
2 teaspoons Dijon mustard
½ teaspoon salt
½ teaspoon freshly ground black pepper
1 egg white, lightly beaten
12 diagonal slices French bread
Dill sprigs, optional garnish

Prepare a medium-hot barbecue fire. Oil the grill rack or coat with a nonstick vegetable spray.

In a mixing bowl, use your hands to combine all of the ingredients except the bread slices and optional dill sprigs. Form into 6 patties, each 3½ to 4 inches in diameter.

Grill the patties, turning once or twice with a spatula just until cooked through, 8 to 10 minutes total. Make sandwiches with the French bread. Garnish with dill sprigs, if desired.

CALORIES	198.18 KCAL	PROTEIN	14.49 GM
TOTAL FAT	4.77 GM	SATURATED FAT	1.63 GM
SODIUM	539.31 MG	CHOLESTEROL	42.63 MG
CARBOHYDRATE	23.03 GM		

% calories from fat: 22.24%

GRILLED VEAL SCALLOPS WITH LEMON AND MARJORAM

4 servings

The delicacy of veal is balanced by a light treatment, such as this one with grilled lemon and herbs served over a bed of fresh pasta. Steamed baby carrots complete a pretty plate.

¼ cup dry vermouth
1 tablespoon fresh lemon juice
2 teaspoons olive oil
1 tablespoon chopped fresh marjoram or 1 teaspoon dried
1 teaspoon grated lemon zest
1 clove garlic, minced
12 ounces veal cutlets, about ¼ inch thick
Salt and freshly ground black pepper
1 small thin-skinned lemon, thinly sliced
4 cups freshly cooked and drained fettuccine
¼ cup chopped parsley
2 tablespoons chopped chives

In a shallow dish just large enough to hold the veal, combine the vermouth, lemon juice, oil, marjoram, lemon zest, and garlic. Season the veal with salt and pepper and place in the marinade, turning to coat completely. Refrigerate 1 hour. Add the lemon slices. Refrigerate 15 minutes more.

Prepare a hot barbecue fire. Oil the grill rack or coat with a non-stick vegetable spray. Grill the veal over the hottest part of the fire and the lemon slices nearer the edge, both 4 to 5 minutes, turning once or twice and brushing with the marinade, until the meat is cooked through and meat and lemon are lightly browned.

Toss the fettuccine with the parsley and chives, then spoon onto a platter or individual plates. Lay the veal over the pasta and top with the grilled lemon slices.

CALORIES	350.39 KCAL	PROTEIN	25.80 GM
TOTAL FAT	6.83 GM	SATURATED FAT	1.56 GM
SODIUM	56.81 MG	CHOLESTEROL	118.50 MG
CARBOHYDRATE	42.70 GM		

% calories from fat: 18.32%

GRILLED PORK TENDERLOIN WITH CABERNET CHERRY SALSA

6 servings

This cherry salsa is a sophisticated accent to the light smokiness of grilled pork tenderloins, which make a lovely main course for summer entertaining. Round the meal out with steamed baby summer squash and a parsleyed rice pilaf.

⅔ cup Cabernet or other dry red wine
2 tablespoons fresh orange juice
2 tablespoons red wine vinegar
2 well-trimmed pork tenderloins (each about 12 ounces)
Salt and freshly ground black pepper
2 cups pitted and halved fresh sweet cherries
¼ cup finely chopped shallots
1 tablespoon grated orange zest
1 tablespoon chopped fresh thyme or 1 teaspoon dried

continued

1 seedless orange, peeled and cut into slices about ¼ inch thick
1 teaspoon vegetable oil, preferably canola oil

In a shallow dish just large enough to hold the pork, combine ⅓ cup of the wine, 1 tablespoon orange juice, and 1 tablespoon vinegar. Season the meat lightly with salt and generously with pepper, then place in the marinade, turning to coat completely. Refrigerate, turning occasionally, 3 to 6 hours.

In a mixing bowl, combine the cherries, shallots, orange zest, and thyme, and the remaining wine, orange juice, and vinegar. Let stand 30 minutes at room temperature or refrigerate up to 12 hours.

Prepare a medium-hot barbecue fire. Lightly oil the grill or coat with a nonstick vegetable spray. Grill the meat, turning once or twice, for a total of about 18 minutes, until the pork is cooked through. Let the meat stand 5 minutes before cutting into diagonal slices. While the meat is resting, brush the orange slices lightly with oil, then grill, turning once, about 4 minutes, until tinged with brown and softened.

For a pretty presentation, arrange the orange slices in a circle on a platter. Lap the meat slices over the oranges and spoon the salsa into the center.

CALORIES	240.60 KCAL	PROTEIN	26.89 GM
TOTAL FAT	6.65 GM	SATURATED FAT	2.05 GM
SODIUM	57.60 MG	CHOLESTEROL	79.94 MG
CARBOHYDRATE	13.57 GM		

% calories from fat: 26.99%

GARLIC AND PEPPER "BOMB" PORK ROAST

ι ι ι ι ι ι ι ι ι

6 servings

The idea for this recipe comes from a smoke pit barbecue in Connecticut, of all unlikely places. The cook/owner pokes holes in a pork shoulder and stuffs them with whole jalapeños and garlic cloves, then smokes the meat for hours. This is a much simpler, quicker, and lower-fat variation, to do at home. Use jalapeños according to your personal heat index. Creamy Picnic Coleslaw (page 155) makes a soothing accompaniment.

½ *cup nonfat plain yogurt*
½ *teaspoon ground cumin*
2 well-trimmed pork tenderloins (each about 12 ounces)
Salt and freshly ground black pepper
4 cloves garlic, minced
1 to 2 jalapeños, finely chopped

In a shallow dish just large enough to hold the pork, stir together the yogurt and cumin.

Butterfly the pork tenderloins by cutting down the length of the meat halfway through, then opening it up like a book. Season all sides of the meat with salt and pepper, then sprinkle the garlic and jalapeños over the cut sides of the meat. Fold the tenderloins back to the original shape and press so that the sides adhere.

Place the tenderloins in the yogurt marinade, turning to coat completely. Refrigerate 1 to 3 hours, returning to room temperature to cook.

continued

Prepare a medium-hot fire. Oil the gril rack or coat with a non-stick vegetable spray. Grill the pork, turning occasionally and brushing with marinade, for a total of 15 to 18 minutes, until cooked through.

Let the meat stand about 5 minutes, then slice and arrange on a platter.

CALORIES	174.72 KCAL	PROTEIN	27.16 GM
TOTAL FAT	5.45 GM	SATURATED FAT	1.92 GM
SODIUM	70.51 MG	CHOLESTEROL	80.31 MG
CARBOHYDRATE	2.53 GM		

% calories from fat: 29.22%

GRILLED PORK TENDERLOINS WITH SMOKED APPLES AND APPLESAUCE

6 servings

Pork and apples are a natural combination, and with the smokiness of the grill added to the equation, it is unbeatable for flavor. Make this for an end-of-the-summer party. Round out the meal with herbed and garlic-seasoned pasta and a tart spinach and escarole salad.

6 tablespoons dry white wine
4 tablespoons Calvados or applejack or apple cider
2 tablespoons reduced-sodium chicken broth
2 well-trimmed pork tenderloins (each about 12 ounces)
1½ teaspoons dried leaf or rubbed sage
Salt and freshly ground black pepper
¾ cup unsweetened applesauce

2 tablespoons prepared horseradish
1 large perfumy apple, such as Golden Delicious
1 teaspoon vegetable oil, preferably canola oil
Sage sprigs, optional garnish

In a shallow dish just large enough to hold the meat, combine 4 tablespoons of the wine, 3 tablespoons of the Calvados, and the broth. Rub the meat with the sage, then season lightly with salt and generously with pepper. Place in the marinade, turning to coat completely. Refrigerate, turning occasionally, 3 to 6 hours.

In a small bowl, combine the applesauce and horseradish, and the remaining wine and Calvados. Season lightly with salt and pepper. Let stand 1 hour at room temperature or refrigerate up to 6 hours.

Prepare a medium-hot barbecue fire. Oil the grill rack or coat with a nonstick vegetable spray. Grill the meat, turning once or twice, for a total of about 18 minutes, until the pork is cooked through. Let the meat stand 5 minutes before cutting into thin diagonal slices. While the meat is resting, core and cut the apple into ¼-inch slices. Brush lightly with the oil, then grill, turning once, for a total of about 4 minutes, until tinged with brown and softened.

To serve, cut each apple slice in half and arrange the pork atop the apple slices. Garnish with fresh sage, if desired.

CALORIES	200.27 KCAL	PROTEIN	22.46 GM
TOTAL FAT	5.53 GM	SATURATED FAT	1.71 GM
SODIUM	60.17 MG	CHOLESTEROL	68.84 MG
CARBOHYDRATE	10.36 GM		

% calories from fat: 27.48%

PORK FAJITAS

~ ~ ~ ~ ~ ~ ~ ~ ~

4 servings

Pork tenderloins make terrific fajitas. A lot of the fat in this popular southwestern "sandwich" comes from the guacamole that is usually spread on the tortillas. Replacing it with seasoned yogurt is a tangy upgrade! Make your own salsa, it's worth the effort.

PORK

2 tablespoons fresh lime juice
2 teaspoons vegetable oil, preferably canola oil
1 teaspoon minced jalapeño
1 well-trimmed pork tenderloin (about 12 ounces)
Salt

CUMIN YOGURT

¾ cup nonfat plain yogurt
¾ teaspoon ground cumin

PICO DE GALLO SALSA

1 cup chopped seeded plum tomatoes
½ cup chopped red onion
½ cup chopped jicama
¼ cup chopped cilantro
1 large clove garlic, minced
1 tablespoon fresh lime juice
1 teaspoon minced jalapeño
Salt

8 flour tortillas

In a shallow dish just large enough to hold the pork, combine the lime juice, oil, and jalapeño. Cut the tenderloin in half crosswise, sprinkle with salt, and add to the marinade, turning to coat completely. Refrigerate 2 to 4 hours, turning occasionally.

Gently stir together the yogurt and cumin. Refrigerate until ready to use.

For the salsa, combine all of the ingredients in a small bowl, seasoning with salt. Refrigerate at least 30 minutes and up to 4 hours.

Prepare a medium-hot barbecue fire. Oil the grill rack or coat with a nonstick vegetable spray. Stack the tortillas and wrap in foil. Grill the pork, turning once or twice, for a total of 15 to 18 minutes, until cooked through. Set the tortilla packet at the edge of the grill for a few minutes to warm.

Thinly slice the pork. Spread the tortillas with some of the cumin yogurt, then divide the pork among the tortillas. Top with some of the salsa and roll up. Serve the remaining yogurt and salsa separately.

CALORIES	402.32 KCAL	PROTEIN	27.45 GM
TOTAL FAT	10.49 GM	SATURATED FAT	2.01 GM
SODIUM	419.52 MG	CHOLESTEROL	56.13 MG
CARBOHYDRATE	48.83 GM		

% calories from fat: 23.63%

Spinach Salad with Grilled Pork Croutons and Shiitake Mushrooms

ₗ ₗ ₗ ₗ ₗ ₗ ₗ ₗ ₗ

6 servings

A little pork goes a long way, as the sesame-coated "croutons" in this sprightly spinach salad inspired by flavors from the Orient attest.

⅓ *cup reduced-sodium chicken broth*
1½ *tablespoons rice vinegar*
1½ *tablespoons fresh lemon juice*
1½ *tablespoons reduced-sodium soy sauce*
1 *large clove garlic, minced*
2 *teaspoons Asian hot sesame oil*
1 *well-trimmed pork tenderloin (about 12 ounces)*
2 *teaspoons sesame seeds*
4 *ounces shiitake mushrooms, trimmed*
1 *yellow or orange bell pepper, cut in 6 wedges*
10 *cups torn spinach leaves*
1 *red onion, thinly sliced*
6 *toasted rice cakes*

In a small bowl, whisk together the broth, vinegar, lemon juice, soy sauce, and garlic. Pour ½ cup of the marinade into a shallow dish just large enough to hold the meat. Add the sesame oil to the remaining liquid in the bowl and reserve to use as the salad dressing. Cut the pork into ¾-inch cubes and place in the marinade, stirring to coat all sides. Let stand 30 minutes at room temperature or refrigerate up to 2 hours.

Prepare a hot barbecue fire. Oil the grill rack or coat with a non-stick vegetable spray. Remove the pork from the marinade, but reserve the marinade for brushing. Thread the pork onto metal skewers, then sprinkle it with the sesame seeds. Thread the mushrooms and bell pepper wedges onto separate metal skewers. Brush each with some of the marinade.

Grill the meat and vegetables, turning once or twice and brushing with more marinade, about 6 minutes, until the meat is cooked through and the vegetables are tinged with brown and somewhat softened.

Place the spinach and onion in a large salad bowl. Toss with the reserved dressing, then spoon out onto serving plates. Remove the meat, pepper, and mushrooms from the skewers. Cut the pepper into thin strips and the mushrooms in slices or halves. Scatter the meat and vegetables over the salad. Garnish the plate with the toasted rice cakes.

CALORIES	177.11 KCAL	PROTEIN	17.66 GM
TOTAL FAT	5.41 GM	SATURATED FAT	1.33 GM
SODIUM	247.04 MG	CHOLESTEROL	39.97 MG
CARBOHYDRATE	15.69 GM		

% calories from fat: 26.73%

Ham and Sweet Potato Kabobs with Redeye Glaze

~ ~ ~ ~ ~ ~ ~ ~ ~

4 servings

Buy high-quality ham, especially the new leaner, reduced-sodium varieties. Redeye gravy is an Appalachian specialty, usually made by stirring coffee and sometimes a touch of molasses into the pan drippings left after frying ham. Here is the same good flavor minus the drippings. The bed of dandelion or other field greens is both attractive and delicious.

1 pound sweet potatoes (about 3)
1 10-ounce piece very lean smoked ham, cut in ¼-inch chunks
1 large sweet onion, cut in 1-inch chunks
3 tablespoons molasses
3 tablespoons strong hot coffee (see note)
1 tablespoon cider vinegar
2 teaspoons Dijon mustard
½ teaspoon dried thyme
6 cups torn young dandelion or other field greens

Prick the sweet potatoes a few times with a fork, then bake in a 350° F. oven about 30 minutes or in a microwave on high power about 5 minutes, until just fork tender. Let cool, then peel and cut them into ¾- to 1-inch chunks. Place the sweet potatoes, ham, and onion in a shallow dish.

In a small bowl, combine the molasses, coffee, vinegar, mustard, and thyme. Pour over the ham and vegetables, stirring to coat completely. Let stand 30 minutes or refrigerate up to 1 hour.

Prepare a hot barbecue fire. Oil the grill rack or coat with a non-stick vegetable spray.

Alternately thread the sweet potatoes, ham, and onion onto 4 metal skewers. Grill, turning once or twice and brushing with the remaining coffee mixture, 7 to 9 minutes, until the meat and vegetables are browned.

On individual plates, make a bed of the greens. Arrange the ham, sweet potatoes, and onion on top.

Note: Make the coffee by dissolving 1 teaspoon instant coffee granules in 3 tablespoons boiling water.

CALORIES	283.94 KCAL	PROTEIN	18.21 GM
TOTAL FAT	4.57 GM	SATURATED FAT	1.18 GM
SODIUM	1,173.31 MG	CHOLESTEROL	33.31 MG
CARBOHYDRATE	44.62 GM		

% calories from fat: 14.06%

DELHI LAMB KABOBS

‍‍‍ ‍ ‍ ‍ ‍ ‍ ‍ ‍ ‍ ‍

4 servings

Yogurt tenderizes meats and forms a protective coating for lean cuts, and its milk proteins promote browning during cooking. Consequently, it is a fine marinade ingredient, a fact long known in India, whose cuisine inspired this recipe.

1 cup nonfat plain yogurt
1 tablespoon fresh lime juice
1 tablespoon minced fresh ginger
1 clove garlic, minced
2 teaspoons ground cumin
¼ teaspoon cayenne
1 pound very lean boneless leg of lamb, cut in 1½-inch cubes
8 small new potatoes
1 green bell pepper, cut in 1-inch strips
1 red onion, cut in 1½-inch chunks

In a shallow dish just large enough to hold the lamb, combine the yogurt, lime juice, ginger, garlic, cumin, and cayenne. Add the lamb and stir to coat completely. Cover and refrigerate at least 2 hours or up to 8 hours. Return to room temperature before cooking.

While the meat is marinating, boil the potatoes in salted water until just tender, about 10 minutes. Drain and reserve.

Prepare a medium-hot barbecue fire. Oil the grill or coat with a nonstick vegetable spray. Alternating the meat and vegetables, thread the lamb, potatoes, bell pepper strips, and onion chunks onto metal skewers. Brush the marinade onto the vegetables.

‍‍‍

Grill, turning occasionally and brushing with the marinade, until the lamb is nicely browned on the outside and pink on the inside, and the vegetables are tender, about 8 minutes total.

CALORIES	282.83 KCAL	PROTEIN	29.47 GM
TOTAL FAT	5.70 GM	SATURATED FAT	1.90 GM
SODIUM	515.85 MG	CHOLESTEROL	73.77 GM
CARBOHYDRATE	27.67 GM		

% calories from fat: 18.33%

GRILLED LAMB KABOBS ON SESAME BUCKWHEAT NOODLES

6 servings

The potent flavors in this teriyaki-style marinade hold up well to the assertiveness of lamb. The sugars in the soy sauce and the sherry give the finished meat a richly caramelized "crust."

1¼ pounds boned and butterflied leg of lamb, trimmed of all fat
½ cup reduced-sodium soy sauce
¼ cup dry sherry
3 cloves garlic, chopped
1 tablespoon Asian hot sesame oil
12 ounces buckwheat noodles, freshly cooked and drained
6 scallions, including green part, chopped
2 slender carrots, thinly sliced into rounds

continued

Cut the lamb into 1-inch pieces.

In a small bowl, combine the soy sauce, sherry, and garlic. Pour half of the marinade into a shallow dish just large enough to hold the lamb. Add the oil to the remainder and reserve it for the pasta. Add the lamb to the marinade, turning to coat completely. Refrigerate at least 2 hours or up to 8 hours.

Prepare a hot barbecue fire. Oil the grill rack or coat with a nonstick vegetable spray. Thread the lamb onto metal skewers. Grill the meat, brushing often with the marinade, until the outside is nicely browned and the meat is cooked to desired degree of doneness, about 8 minutes for medium rare.

Toss the hot pasta with the scallions, carrots, and reserved marinade. Spoon onto a serving platter. Remove lamb from skewers and arrange on pasta.

CALORIES	391.30 KCAL	PROTEIN	29.93 GM
TOTAL FAT	8.63 GM	SATURATED FAT	2.42 GM
SODIUM	672.49 MG	CHOLESTEROL	63.30 MG
CARBOHYDRATE	48.88 GM		

% calories from fat: 19.76%

GRILLED VENISON STEAKS AU POIVRE WITH CUMBERLAND SAUCE

ι ι ι ι ι ι ι ι ι

6 servings

Cumberland sauce is an old standard worth reviving, though today I like to make it a bit more tart than sweet. Particularly well-suited to game, this version of the classic sauce is fat free and a nice counterpoint to the peppery meat. Accompaniments of steamed baby carrots and a wild rice pilaf make a festive presentation.

CUMBERLAND SAUCE

¼ *cup currant jelly*
¼ *cup port wine*
1 *tablespoon red wine vinegar*
¼ *cup finely chopped shallots*
1 *teaspoon cornstarch dissolved in 1 tablespoon cold water*

MEAT AND MARINADE

¼ *cup fresh orange juice*
2 *tablespoons lemon juice*
6 *boneless venison loin steaks (each about 4 ounces and about*
  ¾ *inch thick)*
Salt
1 *tablespoon coarsely ground black pepper*

For the sauce, bring the jelly, wine, vinegar, and shallots to a simmer in a small saucepan set over medium-low heat. Stir almost constantly to melt the jelly. Simmer the sauce gently 3 minutes, then stir the dissolved cornstarch into the sauce and simmer 2 more minutes, until

continued

lightly thickened. (The sauce can be made up to 2 days ahead and refrigerated. Reheat to use.)

In a shallow dish just large enough to hold the meat, combine the orange and lemon juices. Place the meat in the marinade, turning to coat completely. Refrigerate, turning occasionally, 4 to 8 hours.

Prepare a medium-hot barbecue fire. Oil the grill rack or coat with a nonstick vegetable spray. Remove the meat from the marinade. Season lightly with salt, then pat the pepper onto both sides of the meat. Grill the steaks, turning once or twice, until desired degree of doneness, 10 to 12 minutes for medium.

Serve the steaks with the Cumberland sauce.

CALORIES	198.19 KCAL	PROTEIN	26.39 GM
TOTAL FAT	2.78 GM	SATURATED FAT	1.08 GM
SODIUM	65.17 MG	CHOLESTEROL	96.39 MG
CARBOHYDRATE	13.17 GM		

% calories from fat: 13.65%

VEGETABLES

This is my favorite chapter in the book. Fresh vegetables have always been a big part of my family's diet. They became an exciting part of it when I discovered grilled vegetables. Though not difficult to do at home, grilling vegetables is a technique that has come into home-cooking popularity via the restaurant kitchen. To this day, I remember my first taste of a juicy grilled portobello mushroom and my first toasty nibble of grilled corn on the cob. Since then, I have been inspired by the unique flavors of grilled vegetables, and there is hardly a vegetable that I have not successfully cooked on the backyard grill. From asparagus to zucchini, the dictionary of vegetables for grilling is filled with tasty ideas.

Quality is key in grilled vegetables. Buy in season for the best value in both taste and price. Then, for ease in grilling, be sure the vegetables are relatively uniform in size. Tough vegetables, such as potatoes and artichokes, need a short precooking indoors, but this can be done early in the day, leaving only a brief grilling to the last minute. Because they have no natural fat at all, vegetables need to be protected from the flame and from sticking to the grill with a light coating of oil, either alone or as part of a sauce before grilling. To minimize the oil needed, rub it on the vegetables with your fingers instead of brushing.

Because vegetables are delicate and cook quickly, use medium heat for your fire. If you are also cooking meat or poultry, over hotter coals, place the vegetables toward the edge of the grill, where the fire is cooler.

GRILLED BEET AND ORANGE SALAD

ι ι ι ι ι ι ι ι ι

6 servings

I'm not usually a beet fan, but this salad is high on my list of vegetable favorites!

1 bunch beets (about 1 pound)
2 teaspoons vegetable oil, preferably canola oil
6 slices rye bread
2 tablespoons fresh orange juice
1 tablespoon red wine vinegar
2 teaspoons walnut oil
1 tablespoon finely chopped shallots
1 teaspoon grated orange zest
¼ teaspoon salt
⅛ teaspoon freshly ground black pepper
1 head Boston or Bibb lettuce
2 small seedless oranges, peeled and thinly sliced

Prepare a medium barbecue fire. Oil the grill rack or coat with a nonstick vegetable spray.

Trim the beets and cut into slices slightly less than 1/4 inch thick. Rub the slices with the oil.

Grill the beet slices, turning occasionally, until tender and lightly charred, about 12 to 16 minutes. Grill the bread about 30 seconds per side, until lightly toasted. Cut the toasts in quarters.

Whisk together the orange juice, vinegar, oil, shallots, orange zest, salt, and pepper. Make a bed of lettuce on 6 salad plates. Arrange the grilled beet and orange slices in an overlapping circle on each bed of lettuce. Drizzle with the vinaigrette. Garnish with the toast quarters.

CALORIES	146.23 KCAL	PROTEIN	3.77 GM
TOTAL FAT	4.04 GM	SATURATED FAT	.42 GM
SODIUM	282.46 MG	CHOLESTEROL	.00 MG
CARBOHYDRATE	24.71 GM		

% calories from fat: 24.19%

GRILLED ASPARAGUS WITH GREMOLATA VINAIGRETTE

ι ι ι ι ι ι ι ι ι

6 servings

Look for asparagus of consistent medium thickness so that the spears will all cook in approximately the same time. You may either peel the woody part of the stalks with a swivel peeler or simply snap it off at the natural break point.

1 large lemon
1 pound asparagus
1½ tablespoons extra-virgin olive oil
1 clove garlic, minced
6 slices whole wheat bread
2 tablespoons chicken broth
¼ teaspoon salt
¼ teaspoon freshly ground black pepper
3 cups watercress sprigs
2 tablespoons chopped parsley, preferably flat-leaf

continued

Prepare a medium barbecue fire. Oil the grill rack or coat with a nonstick vegetable spray.

Grate 1 teaspoon of zest from the lemon, then cut the fruit in half and squeeze 1 tablespoon of juice from one of the lemon halves. Cut the other half into thin slices. Trim the asparagus. Combine the oil and garlic. Rub the asparagus and lemon slices with about half the flavored oil.

Set the asparagus crosswise on the grill rack and grill, turning occasionally with tongs, until softened and lightly charred, 10 to 12 minutes. Grill the lemon slices, turning once or twice, until softened, 2 to 3 minutes. Grill the bread about 30 seconds per side, until lightly toasted. Cut the toasts into quarters.

Whisk the remaining garlic oil with the lemon juice, broth, salt, and pepper. Arrange the watercress on a platter or individual plates. Place the grilled asparagus and lemon slices on the watercress. Drizzle with the vinaigrette, sprinkle with the parsley, and garnish with the toast quarters.

CALORIES	116.56 KCAL	PROTEIN	4.96 GM
TOTAL FAT	4.22 GM	SATURATED FAT	.67 GM
SODIUM	254.47 MG	CHOLESTEROL	.25 MG
CARBOHYDRATE	16.89 GM		

% calories from fat: 30%

GRILLED JERUSALEM ARTICHOKES

4 servings

Other than a taste similarity, Jerusalem and globe artichokes have nothing in common. Jerusalem artichokes aren't even from Jerusalem, but are the roots of a North American variety of sunflower—hence their other names, of sunchoke and sunroot. They are fabulous when grilled, since the exterior becomes deliciously crunchy and the interior is soft and fluffy like a mashed potato. This is a tasty and unusual vegetable side dish.

1 pound Jerusalem artichokes
2 teaspoons vegetable oil, preferably canola oil
Salt and freshly ground black pepper
2 teaspoons white wine vinegar

Prepare a medium barbecue fire. Oil the grill rack or coat with a non-stick vegetable spray.

Cut or break the unpeeled tubers into chunks about 1½ inches in diameter. Rub all over with the oil. Thread onto metal skewers. Grill the tubers, turning occasionally, for 15 to 20 minutes, until crisp and browned on the outside, and fork tender on the inside.

Season with salt and pepper and splash with the vinegar.

CALORIES	106.70 KCAL	PROTEIN	2.27 GM
TOTAL FAT	2.28 GM	SATURATED FAT	.16 GM
SODIUM	.00 MG	CHOLESTEROL	.00 MG
CARBOHYDRATE	19.87 GM		

% calories from fat: 18.81%

BLACKENED BROCCOLI WITH PENNE AND PARMESAN

ι ι ι ι ι ι ι ι ι

4 to 5 servings

Grilled broccoli is wonderful on its own as a side dish, but when tossed with penne and a little Parmesan, it becomes a fabulous meatless main course. A salad of sliced tomatoes splashed with balsamic vinegar and some crusty bread make this an easy, colorful, and satisfying meal. You can blanch and grill the broccoli a couple of hours ahead of time or add it to the pasta cooking water, then grill it while the pasta is cooking.

2 tablespoons extra-virgin olive oil
3 cloves garlic, minced
¾ cup reduced-sodium chicken broth
¾ cup dry white wine
1 bunch broccoli (about 1 pound)
1 pound penne or other similarly shaped pasta
2 tablespoons grated Parmesan
½ teaspoon freshly ground black pepper
Salt

In a medium skillet, heat 2 to 3 teaspoons of the oil and sauté the garlic over medium-low heat 30 seconds, until it becomes fragrant. Add the broth and wine and simmer 5 to 8 minutes, until reduced by about one third. Take the pan off the heat and reserve.

Prepare a medium barbecue fire. Oil the grill rack or coat with a nonstick vegetable spray. Bring a large pot of lightly salted water to a boil. Trim the broccoli and cut into florets, each with about 1½ inches of stem. Blanch the broccoli about 2 minutes in the boiling water, until the color deepens and the broccoli is barely crisp-tender. Remove with a slotted spoon and transfer to a bowl of cold water to stop the cooking and set the color. Shake the broccoli to rid the florets of excess moisture, then pat dry on paper towels.

Cook the penne in the boiling water about 12 minutes, until al dente. While the penne is cooking, rub the broccoli with the remaining 1 tablespoon olive oil and grill on the rack, turning once or twice, 6 to 8 minutes, until the florets are lightly blackened. Drain the penne and return to the cooking pot. Add the broccoli and the wine sauce. Toss well. Add the cheese, pepper, and salt to taste and toss again.

CALORIES	440.07 KCAL	PROTEIN	14.56 GM
TOTAL FAT	7.98 GM	SATURATED FAT	1.40 GM
SODIUM	156.71 MG	CHOLESTEROL	1.58 MG
CARBOHYDRATE	71.94 MG		

% calories from fat: 17.18%

GRILLED CARROTS WITH GINGER AND HONEY GLAZE

4 servings

I like to buy slim carrots with the tops attached. They taste fresher and sweeter, and grill better than thick carrots. Baby carrots also work well, but they should be skewered or put into a grill basket to keep them from falling through the grill rack. Grilled carrots are wonderful as a side dish to beefsteak or chicken, and make a lovely first course when served atop soft leaf lettuce and sprinkled with chopped chives.

continued

1 *pound slender carrots, trimmed and peeled*
2 *teaspoons vegetable oil, preferably canola*
1 *tablespoon honey*
2 *teaspoons fresh lemon juice*
1 *teaspoon ground ginger*
¼ *teaspoon salt*
⅛ *teaspoon freshly ground black pepper*

Prepare a medium barbecue fire. Oil the grill rack or coat with a non-stick vegetable spray. Rub the carrots with the oil and lay crosswise on the grill rack. Grill, turning occasionally with tongs, until nearly tender, about 18 to 20 minutes.

In a small pan at the edge of the grill, heat the honey, lemon juice, ginger, salt, and pepper until the honey just melts. Brush the carrots with the glaze and continue to grill, turning often and brushing to use all of the glaze, about 5 minutes, until golden brown and tender.

CALORIES	81.90 KCAL	PROTEIN	1.10 GM
TOTAL FAT	2.48 GM	SATURATED FAT	.31 GM
SODIUM	171.32 MG	CHOLESTEROL	.00 MG
CARBOHYDRATE	15.11 GM		

% calories from fat: 25.60%

GRILLED CORN IN THE HUSK

4 servings

This grilling method keeps the corn moist and tender in its own natural "wrapping," and seems to enhance the natural buttery flavor as well. A light brushing with herb-infused oil is a sophisticated touch. Use any herb that complements your meal or mix a combination.

4 ears very fresh corn on the cob
2 teaspoons corn oil
2 teaspoons chopped fresh herbs, such as thyme, marjoram, savory,
  and/or chives
Salt and freshly ground black pepper

Gently pull the husks back from the corn, but do not detach. Pull off and discard the corn silk, then return the husks to their original position, covering the ears. Soak the corn in water to cover 30 minutes.

Prepare a medium barbecue fire. Use tongs to push the hot coals to one side to create indirect heat. Oil the grill rack or coat with a nonstick vegetable spray. Grill the damp corn on the side away from the coals, turning occasionally, 20 to 25 minutes, until the corn kernels are tender.

Discard the husk and brush the corn with the oil. Sprinkle with the herbs, and with salt and pepper.

CALORIES	98.00 KCAL	PROTEIN	2.90 GM
TOTAL FAT	3.34 GM	SATURATED FAT	.44 GM
SODIUM	13.77 MG	CHOLESTEROL	.00 MG
CARBOHYDRATE	17.22 GM		

% calories from fat: 27.19%

GRILLED BELGIAN ENDIVE AND ROASTED PEPPER SALAD

〜 〜 〜 〜 〜 〜 〜 〜 〜

4 servings

These delicate vegetables are simply delicious when grilled. Fanned out over a bed of watercress and draped with strips of roasted red pepper, they also make a very pretty salad.

4 Belgian endives
1 small red bell pepper
1 small yellow bell pepper
1½ tablespoons extra-virgin olive oil
1 tablespoon chopped fresh thyme or 1 teaspoon dried
8 slices French bread
1 bunch watercress
2 tablespoons reduced-sodium chicken broth
1 tablespoon white wine vinegar
1 tablespoon minced shallots
¼ teaspoon salt
¼ teaspoon freshly ground black pepper

Prepare a medium-hot barbecue fire. Oil the grill rack or coat with a nonstick vegetable spray.

Cut the endives in half lengthwise and the bell peppers into quarters. In a small dish, combine the oil and the thyme. Use about half of the oil to rub over all sides of the endives and the peppers. Grill the peppers and the endives, turning occasionally, until tender and lightly charred, 8 to 10 minutes for the peppers and 6 to 8 minutes for the endives. Grill the bread about 30 seconds per side, until lightly toasted.

Divide the watercress among 4 plates. Fan out the grilled endives over the watercress. Cut the grilled peppers into thin strips and drape over the endives.

Whisk the broth, vinegar, shallots, salt, and pepper into the remaining oil mixture. Drizzle over the salads. Garnish with the grilled bread.

CALORIES	103.21 KCAL	PROTEIN	3.13 GM
TOTAL FAT	3.45 GM	SATURATED FAT	.53 GM
SODIUM	240.88 MG	CHOLESTEROL	.00 MG
CARBOHYDRATE	15.41 GM		

% calories from fat: 29.51%

CARAMELIZED LEEKS WITH TARRAGON MUSTARD VINAIGRETTE

ƨ ƨ ƨ ƨ ƨ ƨ ƨ ƨ ƨ

4 servings

Grilled leeks are a real treat. The vinaigrette highlights the sweetness of the vegetable.

6 slender leeks (¾ to 1 inch in diameter)
1½ tablespoons extra-virgin olive oil
1 tablespoon chopped fresh tarragon or 1 teaspoon dried
8 slices French bread
1½ tablespoons white wine vinegar
1½ tablespoons reduced-sodium chicken broth
1 teaspoon Dijon mustard
¼ teaspoon salt

continued

¼ teaspoon freshly ground black pepper
1 large bunch arugula

Prepare a medium barbecue fire. Oil the grill rack or coat with a nonstick vegetable spray.

Wash the leeks well and trim to within 1 inch of the green part, then cut them in half lengthwise if they are more than ¾ inch in diameter. In a small bowl, combine the oil and the tarragon. Rub about half of the flavored oil all over the leeks. Set the leeks crosswise on the grill rack and grill, turning carefully once or twice, 8 to 10 minutes, until softened and lightly charred. Grill the bread about 30 seconds per side, until lightly toasted.

Whisk the vinegar, broth, mustard, salt, and pepper into the remaining oil. Divide the arugula among 4 plates. Cut the leeks cross wise into ½-inch pieces and scatter over the arugula. Drizzle with the vinaigrette. Garnish with the toasts.

CALORIES	134.35 KCAL	PROTEIN	3.69 GM
TOTAL FAT	3.64 GM	SATURATED FAT	.55 GM
SODIUM	267.65 MG	CHOLESTEROL	.00 MG
CARBOHYDRATE	22.58 GM		

% calories from fat: 23.76%

GRILLED PORTOBELLO MUSHROOM SANDWICH

ι ι ι ι ι ι ι ι ι

4 to 6 servings

Portobello mushrooms, though a bit pricey, are as good as a steak in my book. I first tasted a mushroom sandwich at Zoe, a restaurant in New York City. This homemade version is one of my favorite grilled sandwiches.

¼ *cup nonfat or low-fat mayonnaise*
1 *tablespoon chopped fresh rosemary or* ¼ *teaspoon dried*
1 *tablespoon balsamic or red wine vinegar*
3 *cloves garlic, peeled*
2 *teaspoons extra-virgin olive oil*
¾ *pound portobello mushrooms*
Salt and freshly ground black pepper
4 *to 6 sesame seed sandwich rolls, preferably semolina rolls*
1 *ripe tomato, sliced*
1 *small bunch arugula*

Prepare a medium barbecue fire. Oil the grill rack or coat with a non-stick vegetable spray.

In a small dish, stir together the mayonnaise, rosemary, and vinegar. Rub the garlic with about 1 teaspoon of the oil, then wrap the cloves in a double thickness of aluminum foil. Grill at the edge of the coals, turning once or twice, about 15 minutes, until the garlic is very soft. Unwrap and mash or finely chop it and stir into the flavored mayonnaise.

Cut the mushrooms crosswise into diagonal slices slightly less than ½ inch thick. Thread onto metal skewers, then rub the mushrooms with the remaining olive oil. Grill, turning once or twice, about 10 minutes, until the mushrooms are soft and browned. Season with salt and pepper. Split the sandwich rolls, and grill the cut sides about 45 seconds, until lightly toasted.

Assemble the sandwiches by spreading the cut sides of the rolls with the mayonnaise. Layer with the mushroom and tomato slices and the arugula leaves.

CALORIES	213.92 KCAL	PROTEIN	7.25 GM
TOTAL FAT	5.26 GM	SATURATED FAT	.31 GM
SODIUM	386.59 MG	CHOLESTEROL	2.76 MG
CARBOHYDRATE	35.78 GM		

% calories from fat: 21.57%

VERMICELLI AND GRILLED SHIITAKE SALAD

ι ι ι ι ι ι ι ι ι

4 servings

Chinese noodles come in almost as many varieties as the more common Italian versions and can be substituted for the vermicelli called for in this recipe. If you cook the mushrooms on bamboo skewers, lay the skewered mushrooms over the pasta salad for a dramatic presentation.

2 tablespoons rice wine vinegar
2 tablespoons reduced-sodium soy sauce
1 tablespoon sesame oil
1 tablespoon hoisin sauce
1 tablespoon reduced-sodium chicken broth
1 tablespoon minced ginger
2 cloves garlic, minced
12 ounces vermicelli
8 ounces shiitake mushrooms
2 teaspoons vegetable oil, preferably canola oil
1 cup bean sprouts
1 small red bell pepper, diced
½ cup thinly sliced scallions, including green tops

Prepare a medium barbecue fire. Oil the grill rack or coat with a nonstick vegetable spray. If using bamboo skewers, soak them in cold water at least 30 minutes.

In a small bowl, whisk together the vinegar, soy sauce, sesame oil, hoisin sauce, chicken broth, ginger, and garlic. Cook the vermicelli in a large pot of lightly salted boiling water. Drain and toss with half of the dressing. Let cool 15 minutes.

Trim the mushrooms of woody stems. Thread onto metal skewers or soaked bamboo skewers, and rub the mushrooms with the oil. Grill, turning occasionally, about 10 minutes, until the mushrooms are softened and browned.

In a large bowl, toss the pasta, bean sprouts, bell pepper, and scallion with the remaining dressing. Arrange the grilled mushrooms over the pasta and serve warm or at room temperature.

CALORIES	410.52 KCAL	PROTEIN	13.92 GM
TOTAL FAT	7.37	SATURATED FAT	.87 GM
SODIUM	741.88 MG	CHOLESTEROL	.00 MG
CARBOHYDRATE	72.40 GM		

% calories from fat: 16.11%

ROASTED PEPPER PASTA

4 to 6 servings

Roasting bell peppers is easy, and the process transforms ordinary, though colorful, vegetables into really high-class fare. Here, I omitted red peppers since the tomatoes are the same color, but you can use whatever you like from the pepper rainbow at the market.

1 large green bell pepper
1 large yellow bell pepper
1 medium sweet onion, such as Vidalia
1½ tablespoons extra-virgin olive oil
2 cloves garlic, minced
2 (14½-ounce) cans Italian-style stewed tomatoes
½ cup slivered basil
1 pound fresh or dried fettuccine

continued

Salt and freshly ground black pepper
1½ tablespoons grated Parmesan

Prepare a medium-hot barbecue fire. Oil the grill rack or coat with a nonstick vegetable spray.

Quarter the bell peppers. Slice the onion crosswise slightly less than ½ inch thick. Rub the peppers and onion with 1 tablespoon of the oil.

Grill, turning occasionally, 8 to 10 minutes, until the vegetables are softened and lightly charred.

Meanwhile, heat the remaining ½ tablespoon of oil in a large skillet. Sauté the garlic over medium-low heat 30 seconds. Add the tomatoes and juices and simmer 5 minutes. Slice the roasted peppers about ¼ inch thick and separate the onion into rings. Add to the sauce along with the basil and simmer 5 minutes more.

Cook the pasta in lightly salted boiling water about 2 minutes for fresh and about 12 minutes for dried. Drain well and toss with the sauce. Season with salt and pepper and toss again.

Sprinkle with the cheese.

CALORIES	393.06 KCAL	PROTEIN	14.80 GM
TOTAL FAT	6.95 GM	SATURATED FAT	.88 GM
SODIUM	634.04 MG	CHOLESTEROL	107.93 MG
CARBOHYDRATE	69.84 GM		

% calories from fat: 15.59%

GRILLED PLANTAIN SLICES

ʔ ʔ ʔ ʔ ʔ ʔ ʔ ʔ ʔ

4 servings

Plantains, a starchy, savory cousin of the banana, are a delicious alternative to potatoes or rice. They should be thoroughly cooked, so be sure to slice them thinly enough. Serve hot with grilled pork chops or spicy chicken dishes.

4 plantains
1 tablespoon vegetable oil, preferably canola oil
Salt
Caribbean hot sauce, such as Pickapeppa

Prepare a medium barbecue fire. Oil the grill rack or coat with a non-stick vegetable spray.

Cut off the ends of the plantains, then peel off the skin. Cut lengthwise into ¼-inch slices. Rub the slices with the oil. Grill across the rack, turning once or twice with a spatula, 10 to 12 minutes, until crisp and browned on the outside but tender and cooked through in the middle.

Sprinkle the slices liberally with salt and dribble a few drops of hot sauce over them.

CALORIES	248.49 KCAL	PROTEIN	2.32 GM
TOTAL FAT	4.06 GM	SATURATED FAT	.24 GM
SODIUM	7.16 MG	CHOLESTEROL	.00 MG
CARBOHYDRATE	57.08 GM		

% calories from fat: 13.32%

MOLASSES AND PEPPER GRILLED ACORN SQUASH

ι ι ι ι ι ι ι ι ι

4 servings

Sliced squash are delicious simply glazed and seasoned as in this recipe, but precooked squash halves also grill very nicely. The centers can be filled with a little cranberry sauce or cooked wild rice. The timing is about the same as for the slices.

2 small acorn squash (about 1½ to 2 pounds total)
2 tablespoons molasses
1 tablespoon vegetable oil, preferably canola
1 tablespoon fresh orange juice
1 teaspoon grated orange zest
½ teaspoon salt
½ teaspoon coarsely ground black pepper

Prepare a medium barbecue fire. Oil the grill rack or coat with a nonstick vegetable spray.

Cut the unpeeled squash crosswise into slices slightly less than ½ inch thick. Use a biscuit cutter or a small sharp knife to remove the center seeds. Place the slices, slightly overlapping, in a 9- by 13-inch baking dish. Add about ½ cup water and cover the dish with plastic wrap. Microwave 6 to 9 minutes, rotating the slices once, until the squash is just fork tender, not mushy. Or bake the squash in 350° F. oven in a covered baking dish about 20 minutes, until just fork tender.

In a small dish, combine the molasses, oil, orange juice and zest, salt, and pepper. Brush the cut sides of the squash with the molasses mixture.

Grill, turning once or twice with a spatula and brushing with any remaining glaze, 4 to 6 minutes, until the squash is golden brown and glazed.

CALORIES	120.70 KCAL	PROTEIN	1.24 GM
TOTAL FAT	3.56 GM	SATURATED FAT	27.00 GM
SODIUM	281.89 MG	CHOLESTEROL	.00 MG
CARBOHYDRATE	23.47 GM		

% calories from fat: 24.48%

Spicy Grilled Green Tomatoes

≀ ≀ ≀ ≀ ≀ ≀ ≀ ≀ ≀

4 servings

At the end of the summer when my tomato plants don't seem to know how to quit, I often grill green tomatoes and ladle them with home-made red tomato sauce. You can buy unripe green tomatoes (just look for the hard-as-a-rock pale pink ones so often found in the produce bins) any time of the year, and you can substitute canned seasoned stewed tomatoes or bottled marinara sauce for homemade tomato sauce. These tasty green tomatoes can stand alone as a vegetarian main course, and they are a good side dish to simple grilled meats or poultry.

⅓ *cup all-purpose flour*
⅓ *cup yellow cornmeal*
1 *teaspoon dried thyme*
½ *teaspoon salt*
½ *teaspoon freshly ground black pepper*
¼ *teaspoon cayenne*
2 *egg whites*
1 *teaspoon vegetable oil, preferably canola oil*
1 *pound green tomatoes*
2 *cans Cajun-style stewed tomatoes or 2 cups bottled spicy marinara*
   sauce (see note)

In a shallow dish, combine 3 tablespoons of the flour, the cornmeal, thyme, salt, pepper, and cayenne. In another shallow dish, whisk the egg whites until frothy. Whisk the oil into the egg whites. Cut the tomatoes into ½-inch slices. Gently squeeze out the seeds and pat the slices dry. Dust the tomatoes with the remaining flour, then dip in the egg white, then finally into the cornmeal mixture to coat. Set the slices on a rack to dry about 15 minutes.

Prepare a medium barbecue fire. Oil the grill rack or coat with a nonstick vegetable spray. Grill the tomatoes, turning once carefully with a spatula, until golden brown and crisp on the outside and softened on the inside, about 12 minutes total.

Meanwhile, heat the stewed tomatoes or marinara sauce. Serve the tomatoes with the sauce spooned over.

Note: If Cajun-style stewed tomatoes are not available, simmer regular stewed tomatoes with 2 teaspoons chili powder 5 minutes. Season with a dash of Tabasco sauce.

CALORIES	186.89 KCAL	PROTEIN	7.18 GM
TOTAL FAT	1.66 GM	SATURATED FAT	.14 GM
SODIUM	1,037.04 MG	CHOLESTEROL	.00 MG
CARBOHYDRATE	37.12 GM		

% calories from fat: 7.77%

COUSCOUS AND GRILLED VEGETABLE "GREEK" SALAD

≀ ≀ ≀ ≀ ≀ ≀ ≀ ≀ ≀

4 to 6 servings

The mix of crunchy raw vegetables contrasts with the smoky grilled vegetables to give this salad character. Fresh mint and feta add a Greek twist. Pita breads and a poached fruit dessert complete the theme.

1½ *cups dried couscous*
½ *teaspoon salt*
¼ *teaspoon freshly ground black pepper*
1 *large red bell pepper*
1 *large yellow or orange bell pepper*
1 *large red onion*
1 *medium zucchini*
1½ *cups drained and rinsed canned chickpeas*
3 *tablespoons chopped Greek olives*
¼ *cup crumbled feta*
½ *cup chopped mint*
⅔ *cup bottled low-oil or no-oil vinaigrette*
1 *tablespoon extra-virgin olive oil*
Romaine lettuce leaves
Salt and freshly ground black pepper

Prepare a medium barbecue fire. Oil the grill rack or coat with a non-stick vegetable spray.

Place the couscous in a large mixing bowl with the salt and pepper. Pour 2½ cups boiling water over the couscous. Stir to combine, then cover the bowl and let the couscous stand about 5 minutes to soften and absorb the water.

Cut the bell peppers, onion, and zucchini in half. Coarsely chop half of the vegetables and add to the couscous along with the chickpeas, olives, feta, mint, and the vinaigrette. (The salad may be prepared up to 3 hours ahead to this point and refrigerated. Return to room temperature and toss again to fluff before serving.)

Cut the remaining peppers in half again. Slice the zucchini lengthwise and the onion into rings slightly more than ¼ inch thick. Rub the sliced vegetables with the oil. Grill, turning once or twice, until the vegetables are softened and lightly charred, about 8 to 10 minutes for the peppers and onions, and 4 to 7 minutes for the zucchini. Thinly slice the peppers and zucchini, and separate the onion into rings.

Serve the couscous salad on a bed of romaine lettuce with the grilled vegetables arranged on top. Season the grilled vegetables with salt and pepper to taste.

CALORIES	375.40 KCAL	PROTEIN	12.74 GM
TOTAL FAT	8.05 GM	SATURATED FAT	1.74 GM
SODIUM	616.90 MG	CHOLESTEROL	6.00 MG
CARBOHYDRATE	62.30 GM		

% calories from fat: 19.44%

ACCOMPANIMENTS AND DESSERTS

$\mathbb{W}$hile writing this book, I became intrigued with trying to lower the fat in such favorite American barbecue accompaniments as baked beans, potato salad, and cole slaw, as well as traditional summer cookout desserts like strawberry shortcake and berry cobblers. After all, it seemed silly to get smart on the grill, then go over the edge with the rest of the meal. The good news is that the luscious fresh ingredients of summer take beautifully to a lightened treatment.

Salad dressings and buttery pastries were the biggest hurdles. A good bit of tinkering with the ingredient proportions in a vinaigrette, and the replacement of some of the oil with flavored liquids such as broth and fruit juice, resulted in deliciously light and flavorful dressings for coleslaw. High-quality low-fat mayonnaise and sour cream are now readily available and form the basis for an unbelievably creamy dressing for old-fashioned potato salad. Biscuits for shortcake and cobbler toppings are absolutely delicious with a lot less butter than seems possible. The same goes for a wonderfully moist cornbread enriched with the tang of yogurt instead of sour cream.

Fruits, nature's sweets, are elevated to a sophisticated dessert category when pureed and frozen into a simple sorbet or lightly cooked to form a brilliant English summer pudding.

These recipes are plenty good even when you aren't firing up the grill for supper.

≀≀≀

Better Than Grandma's Potato Salad

ι ι ι ι ι ι ι ι ι

10 servings (about 8 cups)

The creamy, tangy dressing here is a pretty darned good facsimile of
Grandma's. Serve it proudly at any picnic, especially one in which
hamburgers, frankfurters, or barbecued ribs are the main course.

2 pounds red potatoes
2 tablespoons nonfat sour cream
1 medium green bell pepper, chopped
½ cup thinly sliced celery
⅓ cup thinly sliced scallions
¼ cup low-fat mayonnaise
¼ cup nonfat plain yogurt
3 tablespoons pickle relish
1½ tablespoons Dijon mustard
½ teaspoon salt
¼ teaspoon freshly ground black pepper
2 tablespoons chopped parsley

Cut the unpeeled potatoes into rough 1½- to 2-inch chunks. Cook in a
large pot of lightly salted boiling water about 10 minutes, until tender.
Drain well and turn into a mixing bowl. Use a small knife to cut each
chunk in half. Add the sour cream to the warm potatoes and toss. Let
cool to room temperature, then add the bell pepper, celery, and scallions to the bowl.

In a small bowl, whisk together the mayonnaise, yogurt, pickle
relish, mustard, salt, and pepper. Pour over the vegetables and toss
gently but thoroughly to coat well.

Refrigerate at least 1 hour or up to 8 hours before serving sprinkled with the parsley.

CALORIES	108.13 KCAL	PROTEIN	2.49 GM
TOTAL FAT	1.97 GM	SATURATED FAT	.40 GM
SODIUM	261.40 MG	CHOLESTEROL	2.09 MG
CARBOHYDRATE	20.17 GM		

% calories from fat: 16.36%

ARIZONA FOUR-BEAN SALAD

ι ι ι ι ι ι ι ι ι

10 to 12 servings (about 7 cups)

It's the jalapeño and cumin that give this salad its Southwest twist. The four different beans give it its colorful character. You can cook your own black beans and use fresh lima beans or use the convenience items listed, but be sure to use only fresh green and wax beans. I especially like this bean salad with grilled pork roasts or fish steaks.

8 ounces fresh green string beans
8 ounces fresh yellow string or wax beans (see note)
1 (10-ounce) package frozen baby lima beans
1 (15- or 16-ounce) can black beans
1 medium red onion, coarsely chopped
¼ cup white wine vinegar
2 tablespoons vegetable oil, preferably canola
1½ tablespoons sugar
1 to 2 teaspoons chopped fresh or pickled jalapeños, to taste
1 teaspoon ground cumin
½ teaspoon salt
¼ teaspoon freshly ground black pepper

continued

Trim the string and wax beans and cut into diagonal pieces about 1½ inches long.

Cook the lima beans in a large pot of lightly salted boiling water 3 minutes. Add the green and wax beans and cook another 2 to 3 minutes, until lima beans are tender and green and wax beans are crisp-tender. Drain well in a strainer, then rinse under cold water to stop the cooking and set the color. Turn the beans into a large mixing bowl. Drain the black beans into the strainer and rinse under cold water. Add to the mixing bowl along with the onion.

In a small bowl, whisk together the vinegar, oil, sugar, jalapeños, cumin, salt, and pepper until the sugar is dissolved. Pour the vinaigrette over the beans and toss to coat completely.

Let the beans stand at least 30 minutes or refrigerate up to 4 hours before serving at cool room temperature.

Note: If you can't get wax beans, use additional green string beans.

CALORIES	103.83 KCAL	PROTEIN	4.36 GM
TOTAL FAT	2.85 GM	SATURATED FAT	.32 GM
SODIUM	181.51 MG	CHOLESTEROL	.00 MG
CARBOHYDRATE	16.16 GM		

% calories from fat: 23.80%

CREAMY PICNIC COLESLAW

ι ι ι ι ι ι ι ι ι

12 to 16 servings (about 7 cups)

It's important to make coleslaw at least an hour ahead of serving so that the acid in the dressing can soften the cabbage a bit. This is an old-fashioned type of slaw that's especially good with plain grilled burgers, barbecued chicken, and any of the grilled pork recipes in the book.

4 cups coarsely shredded green cabbage
3 cups coarsely shredded red cabbage
1 cup coarsely grated carrot
1 small onion, finely chopped
⅓ cup nonfat or low-fat mayonnaise
⅓ cup nonfat or low-fat plain yogurt
2 tablespoons cider vinegar
2 teaspoons sugar
¾ teaspoon salt
½ teaspoon celery seeds
½ teaspoon freshly ground black pepper

Place both cabbages, carrot, and onion in a large mixing bowl. In a small bowl, whisk together the mayonnaise, yogurt, vinegar, sugar, salt, celery seeds, and pepper until the sugar is dissolved. Pour the dressing over the vegetables and toss to mix thoroughly.

Let the coleslaw stand at least 1 hour or refrigerate up to 12 hours before serving.

CALORIES	25.89 KCAL	PROTEIN	.92 GM
TOTAL FAT	.09 GM	SATURATED FAT	.00 GM
SODIUM	201.77 MG	CHOLESTEROL	.10 MG
CARBOHYDRATE	5.78 GM		

% calories from fat: 2.93%

Yankee Maple Baked Beans

ι ι ι ι ι ι ι ι ι

10 servings (about 6 cups)

Low-fat turkey bacon gives the slight smokiness to these baked beans. You can use all red kidney beans for a classic appearance, but I like the contemporary look and taste of a variety of beans. There are some excellent-quality canned beans on the market now, and they make this recipe a breeze to prepare. These are a natural with barbecued chicken, and turkey burgers, too.

1 (15- to 16-ounce) can red kidney beans
1 (15- to 16-ounce) can black beans
1 (15- to 16-ounce) can cannellini beans
2 strips turkey bacon, cut in 1-inch pieces
1 large onion, chopped
2 cloves garlic, minced
⅓ cup chicken or vegetable broth or water
2 teaspoons dry mustard
1 teaspoon dried thyme
½ cup catsup
⅓ cup cider vinegar
⅓ cup maple syrup
1 tablespoon Worcestershire sauce
½ teaspoon Tabasco or other hot sauce

Drain all the beans into a strainer and rinse under cold water. Set them aside. Preheat the oven to 325° F.

In a heavy 2- or 3-quart ovenproof saucepan or Dutch oven, cook the bacon over medium heat until the fat is rendered. Stir in the onion and garlic. Add the broth, cover the pan, and cook over low heat about 5 minutes, until the onion is softened. Stir in the mustard and thyme and cook 1 minute. Add the catsup, vinegar, maple syrup,

Worcestershire sauce, and the beans. Stir well and cover the pan.

Bake 1 hour. Stir in the Tabasco sauce just before serving piping hot. (The beans can be cooked a day ahead and reheated for serving.)

CALORIES	146.89 KCAL	PROTEIN	7.30 GM
TOTAL FAT	1.40 GM	SATURATED FAT	.17 GM
SODIUM	409.91 MG	CHOLESTEROL	1.90 MG
CARBOHYDRATE	27.12 GM		

% calories from fat: 8.38%

SCALLION AND BLACK PEPPER CORNBREAD

ι ι ι ι ι ι ι ι ι

12 squares

This fragrant corn bread is best eaten warm soon after baking. Leftovers make great corn bread stuffing.

¾ cup yellow cornmeal
¾ cup all-purpose flour
1 tablespoon sugar
1½ teaspoons cream of tartar
¾ teaspoon baking soda
½ teaspoon salt
½ teaspoon coarsely ground black pepper
1 egg
1 cup nonfat plain yogurt
¼ cup finely chopped scallion, including green part
2 tablespoons skim milk
2 tablespoons vegetable oil, preferably canola oil

continued

Preheat the oven to 425° F. Coat an 8- by 8-inch square baking dish with nonstick cooking spray.

In a large mixing bowl, whisk together the cornmeal, flour, sugar, cream of tartar, baking soda, salt, and pepper. In a small bowl, beat the egg with a whisk, then gently whisk in the yogurt, scallion, milk, and oil until well blended. Add the liquids to the dry ingredients and stir just until thoroughly blended. Spoon batter into the prepared baking dish.

Bake about 20 minutes, until the corn bread is golden brown and begins to pull away from the sides of the baking dish. Cool slightly before cutting into 12 squares.

CALORIES	104.19 KCAL	PROTEIN	3.24 GM
TOTAL FAT	3.00 GM	SATURATED FAT	.32 GM
SODIUM	191.69 MG	CHOLESTEROL	18.12 MG
CARBOHYDRATE	15.74 GM		

% calories from fat: 26.23%

RASPBERRY SORBET

ı ı ı ı ı ı ı ı ı

1½ quarts (6 to 8 servings)

Unless you can pick your own or shop the local farm stands, fresh raspberries in the supermarket are often extraordinarily high in cost for precious little flavor. Frozen berries can be a better value in price and taste, but when thawed they become mushy. When pureed for sorbet, however, the brilliant color and flavor are all that matter. Other summer berries and liqueurs make fabulous sorbets too, but the sugar syrup may need to be adjusted a bit, according to the sweetness of the fruit.

1¾ cups sugar
3 tablespoons fresh lemon juice
1½ tablespoons crème de cassis
3 pints fresh raspberries or 3 (12-ounce) packages (6 to 8 cups) frozen
unsweetened whole raspberries, thawed

Combine 1¾ cups water and the sugar in a 2-quart saucepan. Bring to a boil, stirring to dissolve the sugar. Boil 2 minutes, then remove from the heat. Stir in the lemon juice and crème de cassis. Let cool completely. Chill at least 1 hour or up to 3 days until ready to use.

Puree the raspberries in a food processor, then strain through a fine-meshed sieve into a large mixing bowl. Whisk in the sugar syrup.

Process in an ice-cream or sorbet maker, according to manufacturer's directions. (Or freeze the mixture in a shallow metal pan or ice cube trays until nearly solid. Break into chunks and process until smooth in a food processor.) Spoon the finished sorbet into a freezer container and freeze at least 1 hour or up to 24 hours before serving. If the sorbet has frozen solid, let it soften slightly in the refrigerator 15 to 20 minutes before serving.

CALORIES	259.88 KCAL	PROTEIN	.97 GM
TOTAL FAT	.60 GM	SATURATED FAT	.02 GM
SODIUM	2.04 MG	CHOLESTEROL	.00 MG
CARBOHYDRATE	64.06 GM		

% calories from fat: 2.03%

BLACKBERRY SUMMER SUNDAES

〜 〜 〜 〜 〜 〜 〜 〜 〜

8 servings

This almost instant sundae sauce can be made with strawberries or raspberries, as well as blackberries. It is also excellent spooned over angel food cake.

1½ pints (4 cups) blackberries
3 tablespoons honey, preferably high-quality berry-blossom honey
2 tablespoons blackberry brandy
2 tablespoons orange juice
1 quart nonfat vanilla or lemon frozen yogurt

Pick over and reserve 1 cup of the smallest and most attractive berries. In a food processor, puree the remaining 3 cups berries with the honey, brandy, and orange juice. Strain through a sieve into a mixing bowl, pressing the puree through with the back of a spoon. Use immediately or refrigerate up to 6 hours, but return to cool room temperature for serving.

When ready to serve, stir the reserved whole berries into the sauce. Ladle the sauce over scoops of frozen yogurt.

CALORIES	164.28 KCAL	PROTEIN	2.42 GM
TOTAL FAT	.21 GM	SATURATED FAT	.00 GM
SODIUM	45.34 MG	CHOLESTEROL	.00 MG
CARBOHYDRATE	36.96 GM		

% calories from fat: 1.18%

HUCKLEBERRY COBBLER

ₜ ₜ ₜ ₜ ₜ ₜ ₜ ₜ ₜ

8 servings

Huckleberries are not a cash crop, so to get them you need a pail and a huckleberry patch. However, huckleberry's cousin, the cultivated blueberry, is available far and wide all summer. The berries are interchangeable in this recipe.

FILLING

2 pints huckleberries or blueberries
⅔ cup sugar
1 tablespoon cornstarch
1 teaspoon fresh lemon juice

DOUGH

1½ cups all-purpose flour plus additional flour for rolling the dough
¼ cup plus 1 teaspoon sugar
1½ teaspoons baking powder
1 teaspoon baking soda
¼ teaspoon salt
1½ tablespoons cold unsalted butter, cut in small pieces
¾ cup cold skim-milk buttermilk
1 tablespoon vegetable oil, preferably canola oil
1 teaspoon grated lemon zest

Preheat the oven to 400° F. Coat a deep 9-inch pie plate with nonstick vegetable spray.

For the filling, combine the huckleberries, sugar, cornstarch, and lemon juice in a mixing bowl, stirring to mix thoroughly. Spoon into the prepared pie plate.

continued

For the dough, in a mixing bowl whisk together the flour, ¼ cup of the sugar, the baking powder, baking soda, and salt. Use a pastry blender or two knives to cut in the butter until the mixture is crumbly. In a small bowl, whisk together the buttermilk and oil. Add the zest. Make a well in the center of the dry ingredients and pour in the buttermilk. With a fork, stir just until combined.

Turn the dough out onto a lightly floured surface. Roll or pat to a rough 8-inch circle. Gently lift the dough and set it on the berries. Use your fingers to pinch and patch any tears. (The dough is supposed to look rough and "cobbled.") Use a fork to prick the dough in several places, then sprinkle the top with the remaining 1 teaspoon sugar.

Bake in the center of the oven 25 to 30 minutes, until the fruit bubbles and the dough is golden brown. Cool the cobbler on a rack. Serve warm or at room temperature.

CALORIES	273.05 KCAL	PROTEIN	3.89 GM
TOTAL FAT	4.68 GM	SATURATED FAT	1.62 GM
SODIUM	346.28 MG	CHOLESTEROL	6.73 MG
CARBOHYDRATE	55.48 GM		

% calories from fat: 15.06%

PEACH AND SWEET CHERRY AMBROSIA

ʑ ʑ   ʑ ʑ   ʑ ʑ   ʑ ʑ   ʑ

6 servings

Bing cherries, with their incomparable flavor and ruby red color, are the best choice here. Peaches are my favorite "ambrosial" fruit of summer. Together they make a spectacular presentation. Other color-compatible fruits, such as raspberries and nectarines or strawberries and Queen Anne cherries, are also lovely.

¼ cup honey, preferably a high-quality berry-blossom honey
2 tablespoons fresh lime juice
2 large mint sprigs plus 6 small sprigs for garnish
4 cups peeled and thinly sliced peaches (about 6 peaches)
1½ cups pitted Bing cherries
2 cups chilled Champagne or other sparkling white wine

In a small saucepan, heat the honey, lime juice, and the 2 large mint sprigs over low heat just until the honey melts. Remove from the heat and let steep 10 minutes. Discard the mint sprigs.

Place the peaches and cherries in a mixing bowl. Pour the honey over them and stir gently to combine. Divide the fruit mixture among 6 individual stemmed goblets or glass dessert dishes. Refrigerate up to 1 hour.

When ready to serve, pour the Champagne over the chilled fruit and garnish each dessert with a small mint sprig.

CALORIES	172.93 KCAL	PROTEIN	1.37 GM
TOTAL FAT	.46 GM	SATURATED FAT	.08 GM
SODIUM	5.31 MG	CHOLESTEROL	.00 MG
CARBOHYDRATE	31.28 GM		

% calories from fat: 3.07%

STRAWBERRY SHORTCAKES

4 to 5 servings

Strawberry shortcake is the quintessential American summer dessert. In fact, it probably wouldn't be summer in most parts of the country without at least one serving of strawberry shortcake.

TOPPING
⅔ *cup nonfat vanilla yogurt*
⅓ *cup nonfat sour cream*

BERRIES
1½ *pints strawberries*
⅓ *cup sugar*
1½ *tablespoons light rum or orange juice*

SHORTCAKES
1½ *cups all-purpose flour plus extra for forming the shortcakes*
3 *tablespoons sugar*
1½ *teaspoons baking powder*
1 *teaspoon baking soda*
¼ *teaspoon salt*
1 *tablespoon cold unsalted butter, cut in small pieces*
1 *tablespoon vegetable oil, preferably canola oil*
⅔ *cup skim-milk buttermilk*

For the topping, gently stir together the yogurt and sour cream. Refrigerate until ready to use, up to 24 hours.

In a large mixing bowl, with a fork mash half of the berries, the sugar, and the rum. Slice the remaining berries and add to the bowl.

Stir to combine. Let stand at least 30 minutes or refrigerate up to 4 hours before using.

For the shortcakes, preheat the oven to 425° F. Coat a baking sheet with nonstick vegetable spray.

In a mixing bowl, whisk together the flour, all but 1 teaspoon of the sugar, the baking powder, baking soda, and salt. Use a pastry blender or two knives to cut the butter into the flour until crumbly. Make a well in the center and pour in the oil and all but 2 teaspoons of the buttermilk. With a fork, stir just until combined to make a slightly sticky dough. Do not overmix.

Turn the dough out onto a lightly floured surface. Knead 10 times, then pat or roll to an even 1-inch thickness. Using a 2½- or 3-inch round biscuit cutter, cut out shortcakes and transfer to the prepared baking sheet, leaving about 2 inches between them. Brush the tops of the shortcakes with the reserved 2 teaspoons buttermilk and sprinkle with the reserved 1 teaspoon sugar.

Bake the shortcakes in the center of the oven 12 to 16 minutes, until golden. Transfer to a rack and let cool slightly. Use a serrated knife to split the warm shortcakes horizontally.

To assemble, place the shortcake bottoms on dessert plates. Spread with some of the yogurt topping. Spoon on the strawberries and juices, and replace the biscuit tops. Dollop with remaining yogurt topping.

CALORIES	362.38 KCAL	PROTEIN	8.53 GM
TOTAL FAT	6.03 GM	SATURATED FAT	2.02 GM
SODIUM	575.21 MG	CHOLESTEROL	8.39 MG
CARBOHYDRATE	66.47 GM		

% calories from fat: 15.31%

English Summer Pudding

〜 〜 〜 〜 〜 〜 〜 〜 〜

6 servings

This make-ahead "pudding" is to England what strawberry shortcake is to the American summer table, especially when it is made with the classic combination of red currants and loganberries. If these are not available, other combinations, such as raspberries and blackberries or blueberries, can be used. Just be sure that at least half of the berries are red, for the pudding to have the prettiest color.

1 pint red currants or raspberries
1 pint loganberries or blackberries
⅔ to ¾ cup sugar, depending upon sweetness of the fruit
¼ cup seedless raspberry or strawberry fruit spread or jam
1 tablespoon raspberry eau-de-vie or framboise
1 teaspoon fresh lemon juice
7 to 9 slices firm white sandwich bread, crusts trimmed
1 cup nonfat vanilla yogurt

In a large heavy saucepan, combine the currants, loganberries, sugar, and 1 tablespoon water. Bring to a simmer, stirring. Simmer over medium-low heat 2 minutes. Remove from the heat, stir in the berry spread or jam, liqueur, and lemon juice. Let cool completely.

Line a 1-quart soufflé dish, pudding basin, or mixing bowl with plastic wrap, leaving a 4-inch overhang all the way around. Cut the bread slices in half diagonally, then fit them in the bottom and sides of the bowl, trimming further to fit snugly if needed. Reserve extra slices for the top.

Spoon the berry mixture into the bread-lined bowl. Trim bread slices level with the top. Use remaining bread to completely cover the top. Fold the plastic wrap in over the top of the pudding, then place a plate slightly smaller in diameter than the top of the bowl directly onto the plastic wrap. Weight the plate with a heavy can. Refrigerate at least 8 hours or up to 24 hours.

To serve, remove the weight and plate, then fold back the overlap of plastic wrap. Place a rimmed serving dish over the pudding, then invert the bowl onto the dish. Remove the bowl and plastic wrap. Carefully cut wedges with a serrated knife and serve each portion with a dollop of yogurt.

CALORIES	300.93 KCAL	PROTEIN	5.72 GM
TOTAL FAT	1.49 GM	SATURATED FAT	.27 GM
SODIUM	215.80 MG	CHOLESTEROL	1.45 MG
CARBOHYDRATE	67.34 GM		

% calories from fat: 4.38%

STUFFED FIGS WITH AMARETTO

~ ~ ~ ~ ~ ~ ~ ~ ~

4 servings

Figs are a late summer and early autumn treat. In Italy, they are often enjoyed with a stuffing of rich mascarpone and an accompaniment of crisp amaretti. Lightly sweetened low-fat cream cheese (Neufchâtel) and nonfat sour cream is a delicious approximation of mascarpone, and the Amaretto is reminiscent of the flavors of the cookies. The filling is also good piped or spooned into fresh apricot or small purple plum halves.

2 ounces (about ¼ cup) softened low-fat cream cheese (Neufchâtel)
2 tablespoons nonfat sour cream
1 tablespoon confectioners' sugar
8 fresh figs or small apricots or purple prune plums
⅛ teaspoon ground cinnamon
2 tablespoons Amaretto

Use a spoon or a small food processor to blend the cream cheese, sour cream, and confectioners' sugar. Make a deep slit in the figs and squeeze gently to open a pocket, or cut the apricots or plums in half and discard the pits.

Spoon the cheese filling into a pastry bag with a plain or star tip, or use a small spoon to fill the fruits. Dust the filling with the cinnamon. Divide among 4 serving plates and drizzle with the Amaretto.

CALORIES	137.08 KCAL	PROTEIN	2.73 GM
TOTAL FAT	2.80 GM	SATURATED FAT	1.55 GM
SODIUM	86.01 MG	CHOLESTEROL	7.49 MG
CARBOHYDRATE	24.83 GM		

% calories from fat: 18.60%

GRILLED BANANA MAPLE RUM SUNDAES

ϱ ϱ ϱ ϱ ϱ ϱ ϱ ϱ ϱ

4 servings

Move over, Bananas Foster. This is delicious served with chocolate or coffee frozen yogurt.

⅓ cup plus 1 tablespoon maple syrup
1½ tablespoons dark rum
1 tablespoon melted unsalted butter
4 ripe but firm bananas
1 pint low-fat or nonfat vanilla frozen yogurt
⅛ teaspoon freshly ground nutmeg

Prepare a medium barbecue fire. Oil the grill rack or coat with a nonstick vegetable spray.

In a small saucepan, combine ⅓ cup maple syrup and the rum. In a small dish, combine 1 tablespoon maple syrup and the melted butter. Peel the bananas and cut in half lengthwise. Brush or rub the bananas with the maple syrup and butter mixture. Grill the bananas, turning once or twice with a spatula, 3 to 5 minutes, until the fruit is lightly browned and softened but not mushy. While the bananas are grilling, heat the maple syrup and rum in a small saucepan set at the edge of the coals.

Scoop the frozen yogurt into dessert dishes. Cut the banana halves into quarters and place on the frozen yogurt. Pour the warm sauce over them. Sprinkle with the nutmeg.

CALORIES	320.82 KCAL	PROTEIN	6.79 GM
TOTAL FAT	4.90 GM	SATURATED FAT	2.91 GM
SODIUM	108.19 MG	CHOLESTEROL	13.43 MG
CARBOHYDRATE	63.33 GM		

% calories from fat: 13.58%

INDEX

〜 〜 〜 〜 〜 〜 〜 〜 〜